THE ART AND THOUGHT
OF JOHN

THE ART AND THOUGHT OF JOHN

J. EDGAR BRUNS

HERDER AND HERDER

1969
HERDER AND HERDER
232 Madison Avenue, New York, N.Y. 10016

CONTENTS

ABBREVIATIONS

AER:	*American Ecclesiastical Review*
Bibl:	*Biblica*
BJRylL:	*Bulletin of the John Rylands Library*
CBQ:	*Catholic Biblical Quarterly*
CSCO:	*Corpus Scriptorum Christianorum Orientalium*
CSEL:	*Corpus Scriptorum Ecclesiasticorum Latinorum*
EB:	*Enchiridion Biblicum*
ExpTim:	*Expository Times*
HarvTR:	*Harvard Theological Review*
HeythJ:	*Heythrop Journal*
JBL:	*Journal of Biblical Literature*
JRAS:	*Journal of the Royal Asiatic Society*
JTS:	*Journal of Theological Studies*
MPG:	Migne: *Patrologia Graeca*
MüTZ:	*Münchener Theologische Zeitschrift*
NedTTs:	*Nederlands Theologisch Tijdschrift*
NovT:	*Novum Testamentum*
NRT:	*Nouvelle Revue Theologique*

NTS:	*New Testament Studies*
PO:	*Patrologia Orientalium*
RB:	*Revue Biblique*
RechSR:	*Recherches de Science Religieuse*
RevBen:	*Revue Benedictine*
Revue de l'Hist. *des Rel.:*	*Revue de l'Histoire des Religions*
Script:	*Scripture*
TS:	*Theological Studies*
ZNW:	*Zeitschrift für die Neutestamentliche* *Wissenschaft*

To my students, friends,
and colleagues in Toronto
*"in qua urbe et hospitiolum
et amicos amantissimos sui habebat"*
(Eusebii Pamphili *Chronici Canones*)

PREFACE

I have been fascinated by the gospel and epistles of John since I was a student in high school, so that in one sense it might be said that this book has been in process for more than thirty years. In retrospect it is easy to see the various stages of appreciation and understanding of them through which I have passed and the reasons for the changing appreciation. One of the most recent and surely one of the most exciting works to deal with Johannine thought is Ernst Käsemann's *Jesu letzter Wille nach Johannes 17 (The Testament of Jesus)*. If his thesis is correct, which I do not personally think it is, my very naïve understanding of the gospel thirty years ago was essentially the correct one. His book challenged me to set in order my own views on this enigmatic gospel, a project which I had in any case been contemplating for the past several years.

I have endeavored to read every important commentary, study, and article on the Johannine literature (the gospel and the three epistles), though inevitably there have been

11

oversights. I have also, inevitably, been influenced in one way or another by the opinions of others, just as I am indebted to them for the development of my own. But it is from the text of the gospel and the epistles themselves that I have drawn whatever original insights there may be in what I have to say.

When a great deal has been written on a particular topic, as in this case, it is difficult to know how much of that volume of literature should be reproduced in condensed form. If one's aim is primarily to present the basic thought of a writer, but to present it from what is felt to be an original perspective, it becomes necessary to repeat a good deal of what may already be known to the reader— although from the same, purportedly new, perspective. If a man's thought is highly sophisticated, then his manner of expressing it, his literary art, and his life experience ought also to be such. With this conviction, it has been my aim in the first and third parts of this volume to look at the gospel as a piece of writing and at the author as a man. But those familiar with the mountain of published material on John will be more interested in the central part of the book which is the fruit of my own reflection on the Johannine gospel and epistles. I often strike a Bultmannian note, but at no point did my interpretation of John stem from that exegete's premises or exposition.

In suggesting as I do that John's thought shows some *structural* affinity to Mahayana Buddhism, I am certain to incur criticism, but it will be welcomed if it at least calls attention to the need for further study along these lines. Certainly it cannot be denied today that the influence of

12

Indian philosophy on the intellectual milieu of the Mediterranean world in the first century of our era was greater than anyone could have imagined a century ago, and this gospel is the Christian masterpiece of that world.

For assistance in various ways and at various stages in the composition of this book, my thanks are due to Professor Morton Smith of Columbia University, to my colleagues Professors Leslie Dewart and Joseph O'Connell, and to my former students, especially Messers Henry A. Schankula and Michael J. O'Halloran.

Part One:
THE BOOK AND ITS FORMATION

Current Interest in the Gospel of John

It is no exaggeration to say that the interest shown in the fourth gospel over the past twenty years has been phenomenal. Some of the most brilliant biblical commentaries and studies of the century deal with this gospel—those of Hoskyns, Bultmann, Dodd, Barrett, Lightfoot, Brown,[1] Schnackenburg,[2] Käsemann—and there is no end in sight to the continuing flow of contributions.[3] The last words of the gospel, if applied to this prodigious output of literature on it, are entirely appropriate: "I think that not even the world itself would hold the books being written" (Jn. 21, 25).

Of course, it is no new thing for the Gospel of John to enjoy special attention. It was much loved and much used by the Fathers of the Church [4] and by Christians generally down to the Age of Enlightenment. But with the rise of modern biblical scholarship the fourth gospel fell into a kind of disrepute. Viewed from the standpoint of a rigid historicism which did not at that time have anywhere near enough evidence to make the judgments it did, the fourth gospel was shunted aside as the late work (second century) of a thoroughly Hellenistic Christian who had no firsthand experience of Jesus and no reliable secondhand information at his disposal either. The striking differences between his work and the Synoptics showed that he was not in any case even interested in historicity. The gospel was useful perhaps as a book of meditations, but it was useless as a "source" for the life and teaching of Jesus. This rather contemptuous estimate of John [5] prevailed for more than a century, but as is well known today, its premises have had gradually to be abandoned. Papyri recently come to light have pushed the latest possible date for the gospel's composition back to the period traditionally maintained: the end of the first century. Linguistic, stylistic, and comparative studies have shown that, while remaining highly original in his work, John is nevertheless very truly an heir of two cultures: the Judaic and the Hellenistic. If some of his topographical references remain obscure, others have been demonstrated to reflect a remarkable accuracy.[6] But perhaps the most important factor contributing to the rehabilitation of the fourth gospel is the new understanding about the origin and nature of the gospels. The nineteenth-century critics canonized Mark as the "primitive gospel," by which they meant the gospel which made the greatest use of trustworthy secondhand accounts of Jesus and his teaching and which, accordingly, provided the best outline of his public life. It was thought to be as free as could be expected of any slanting. Everything that was considered to be true of Mark was found wanting in John. But today, largely as a result of the methods of Form Criticism applied to the New Testament, such a designation as "most primitive gospel" is seen to be meaningless. All of the gospels make use of the same source material, which had its own prehistory, but each of them utilizes it in a distinctive manner; each evangelist has his own theological perspective, and it is that perspective which the exegete must understand. The history of "gospel redaction" is, consequently, the primary concern of contemporary gospel exegetes. John has been freer with his material than the other evangelists, no doubt, but the importance of that fact is subordinate to the question arising from it: Why?

Basically, of course, the answer is that John, as much as Matthew, Mark, or Luke, wants to present the *meaning* of the words of Jesus and of the stories about him with which he was familiar. How he goes about this reveals his craftsmanship as much as it does his theology. And this leads us closer to a satisfactory explanation of why John enjoys so much popularity today. The fact that the gospel itself can now be credited with as much value as the others is no sufficient reason. The explanation lies in the quality of John's work. Again, we have come full circle, for the ancients gave to John alone among the evangelists the title *"theologos,"* "the theologian." John is pre-eminently a theologian; he is also a consummate artist. Part of his art—and a large part of his attractiveness to the exegete— is the over-all impression given of great simplicity, under which actually lie waiting to be discerned intricate patterns of thought. In Part Two of this study we shall have occasion to see how much patient unraveling and correlating of the evangelist's paragraphs is required in order to get at the meaning of his keywords. He repeats these words so often that the unwary reader is apt to come under the illusion that he understands what is being said merely because certain phrases become so familiar, but like the Jesus of his pages (Jn. 5, 13; 6, 15; 8, 59; 10, 39; 11, 54; 12, 36), the evangelist frequently hides himself. In this respect much can also be missed, indeed the whole point of an episode,[7] by failure to appreciate the evangelist's love for symbolism. This was not missed by the great commentators of John in antiquity such as Origen, Cyril of Alexandria, and Augustine; indeed they must at times be charged with an over-sensitivity to it. Nor is it missed by the majority of modern scholars, although some dismiss it,[8] at the risk perhaps of falling into the kind of lifeless, pedantic, and even occasionally obtuse interpretation characteristic of Theodore of Mopsuestia.[9] John does not have to declare his intention (as he does, for example, at 9, 7) every time he employs symbolism. The care with which he sets his scenes is sufficient indication. Who can doubt, for instance, that in drawing attention to Jacob's well in chapter 4, at which Jesus speaks of giving water that will become a spring welling up for eternal life (Jn. 4, 14), John is consciously alluding to the Jewish legend of Jacob and the well of Haran?[10] Jacob was responsible for that well yielding an abundance of water for twenty years. Jesus gives the water of the Spirit which will never fail. The fact that John's details are always capable of a symbolic meaning[11] does not mean that they have been chosen arbitrarily and independently of authentic tradition, but rather that

20

he has with a certain freedom selected only those which enable him to emphasize his particular hermeneutic.

In the course of the ensuing discussion of the gospel's formation, we will note other and different examples of John's subtle artistry. To understand the evangelist's temperament is as important as to understand his rather simple Greek, for, as M. F. Wiles rightly observes, this gospel reveals its secrets more readily to "a certain intuitive sympathy of understanding" [12] than to critical methods.

The Formation of the Gospel

I. THE RELATION OF THE GOSPEL
TO THE THREE JOHANNINE EPISTLES

Something must be said at this point about the three
epistles attributed to John. That the same man responsible
for the fourth gospel was also the author of these epistles
seems evident to the ordinary reader, and so, for the most
part, it has rested. If one turns from the gospel to the
first epistle, he will be immediately struck by the similarities
of style and thought; in fact, it will appear that the discourses of Jesus in the gospel are couched in the phraseology of the man who wrote the epistle. Since the character
of the gospel is unmistakable, it could hardly be doubted
that the epistle derived from the same source. The two
shorter epistles also betray a marked resemblance to the
longer Johannine works, and since they are of no great
doctrinal significance, it is difficult to believe that anyone
in antiquity would have bothered to fabricate them.

However, no less an authority on John than C. H. Dodd

challenged the unity of authorship just over twenty years ago.[13] He reasoned that in thought, and even in vocabulary, the gospel and the first epistle stood sufficiently apart to warrant serious doubt about a common single author. On the other hand, he made it very clear that, so far as he was concerned, the author of the epistles, though not the evangelist, was someone very close to the latter, undoubtedly a disciple. Although most of his arguments were dealt with rather effectively a year later by W. F. Howard,[14] the kind of unanimity of opinion which previously existed had now been brought to an end.

In this study, however, it will be assumed that the author of gospel and epistles is one and the same. Linguistically, all the differences between the gospel and the epistle can be explained most reasonably on the basis of the one being a narrative about Jesus which includes lengthy discourses, and the other being a letter (letters) to a Christian community in which Jesus is occasionally mentioned.[15] Doctrinally, the differences are largely imaginary. Dodd asserts that the eschatology of the gospel is more advanced than that of the epistle. As we shall see when we deal with John's eschatology, the twofold eschatology, realized and futurist, is present in both. Actually, the epistle is more advanced in this respect than the gospel. Dodd also finds the epistle empty of the gospel's "high" doctrine of the Spirit. But it can be said, on the other hand, that the epistle develops very much more than does the gospel the very sophisticated Johannine concept of God as Love. Dodd's final objection, that the epistle presents a theology of atonement which, when compared with the exalted soteriol-

23

ogy of the gospel, can only be considered crude, more or less assumes that the epistle's two passing references to Jesus as the "expiation" for our sins (1 Jn. 2, 2; 4, 10) are an exhaustive statement of the writer's thought. The treatment of sin in 1 Jn. 3, 4-10 and the relationship it establishes between the absence of sin and abiding in Christ is far more relevant (cp. Jn. 8, 34-47).

It has been necessary to say at least this much about the relationship between the fourth gospel and the Johannine epistles because the first of these letters will be cited frequently as being the work of the evangelist, and as being in some respects a fuller and more penetrating exemplar of his theological intuitions.

II. THE ORGANIZATION OF THE MATERIAL IN THE GOSPEL

It has already been remarked that John is fond of repeating favorite words and phrases. It will be seen that he also, while making use of different incidents and characters, keeps repeating his few basic premises about Jesus and his teaching. The pattern of almost every episode bears an unmistakable similarity to some other. This can sometimes lead to the impression that the gospel is an assemblage of material lacking any plan of organization and cohesive only insofar as it all deals with the significance of Jesus. This it is not.

An attentive reading of the gospel will show that the material in it has been arranged to follow a liturgical calendar. From chapter 2 to chapter 19 inclusive, the background of the events and of the dialogue is specified as being one or another of the feasts of the Old Law. Passover is the backdrop for the section 2, 13—3, 22; an unnamed feast, probably Pentecost,[16] for chapter 5; Passover again for chapter 6; Tabernacles (Booths) for the central section 7 to 9; Hanukkah (Dedication) for chapter 10; and a final Passover (first mentioned at 11, 55 and then again at 12, 1; 13, 1; 18, 28. 39) for chapters 11 through 19. There is no stated festal background for the introductory section (1, 19—2, 11), for chapter 4, nor for the final two chapters, but they are not without liturgical overtones. Chapter 4 is set in Samaria (4, 3–42) and Samaria was beyond the pale of Jewish orthodoxy; it was, so to speak, a liturgical "no-man's land" (cf. Jn. 4, 22), and we should not, therefore, expect to find any reference to a Jewish festival. Nevertheless, the question of worship occupies an important place in the dialogue between Jesus and the Samaritan woman (4, 19–24), and it is here that Jesus impugns the notion of any exclusive localization of cult. The introductory section is carefully divided into days which total either six or seven. If the number is seven, as has been well argued,[17] we would have here an inaugural week, the week of the new creation in which Jesus lays the foundations of the Christian community.[18] If the number of days is six, which seems less likely, John may intend a parallel with the Greek liturgical calendar.[19] In either case, the last day is also "the third day" (2, 1), the religious connotations of which, for Christian ears, were obvious (Acts 10, 40). In the last section of the gospel, chapters 20 and 21, a distinction must be made between the chap-

25

ters. The second of the two is widely regarded today as an appendix written by the evangelist's disciples.[20] Our concern then is with chapter 20. It is John who calls to our attention the fact that the final scene takes place eight days after the Resurrection (20, 26). This would again be a Sunday. From subapostolic times we find references in Christian writings to the eighth day;[21] the Christian "week," in superseding the Jewish, had added another day, the Lord's day on which it commemorated his Resurrection at the eucharistic gathering (Acts 20, 7). Accordingly, it is not impossible that John, having opened the gospel with a new week of seven days, concludes it with a final week of eight days to indicate that the inauguration of the Christian era has been completed.

The significance the evangelist attached to his liturgical framework—the existence of which for chapters 2 to 19 cannot be questioned—is brought out more clearly by seeing how, generally, the narrative or the discourse material accords with the feast which provides the background for it:

Jn. 4, 3–42. Samaria. No feast. Location: Mt. Gerizim (4, 20), site of the ruined Samaritan temple.

Jesus speaks of worship "in spirit and truth." He rejects the idea of any exclusive localization of cult.

Jn. 5. "A feast of the Jews" (5, 1), probably Pentecost, which commemorated the giving of the Law.[22]

Narrative and discourse turn on the Law. Does Jesus violate it or do the Jews? Specific reference at 45–47.

Jn. 6. Passover (6, 4), which commemorated the Exodus and

"Your fathers ate the manna in the wilderness yet they died"

26

God's providence for the Jews in the wilderness.

(6, 49). Jesus is the true bread of life.

Jn. 7—9. Tabernacles (7, 2), a prefiguring of the messianic era. The principal ceremonies were the solemn drawing of water from the pool of Siloam and subsequent libation, and the illumination of the Temple.

Is Jesus the Messiah (7, 26. 41)? Jesus is the source of living water (7, 37–38) and the light of the world (8, 12). The blind man recovers his sight at the pool of Siloam, which is a figure of Jesus (9, 7).

Jn. 10. Hanukkah (Dedication, 10, 22), which commemorated the reconsecration of the Temple after it had been defiled by pagans and the unworthy priests Jason and Menelaus.

Jesus is the good shepherd (10, 11. 27). Jesus has been consecrated by the Father (10, 36).

Jn. 13—19. Passover, the principal rite of which was the sacrifice and eating of the paschal lamb.

Jesus prepares his disciples for his departure. He dies on the cross as the true paschal lamb (Jn. 19, 33–36).

The exceptions (2, 13—3, 36 and chapters 11—12) to what is clearly the rule call for an explanation which will be given when we examine the state of the gospel as we have it.

Before continuing with further evidence of John's conscious effort to organize his material, there is more to learn from the structuring of this gospel around the Jewish liturgy than a simple plan of organization. It tells us, for one thing, that John saw in Jesus the fulfillment of Israel's cult. In Jesus the worship of God is perfected, and consequently any ritual will be meaningless which is not an extension of the word and presence of Jesus. This the

Christian sacraments are and, accordingly, John alludes to them in his gospel. To what extent is a hotly debated question today,[23] but apart from arbitrary dissections of the text, it can hardly be doubted that he has baptism in mind at 3, 5; 9, 7; and probably 7, 37–38, and the Eucharist at 6, 48–58. Both may be intended at 19, 34.

For another, it strongly suggests, to say the least, that he had been himself a priest or Levite. In the whole of the New Testament only the epistle to the Hebrews shows an interest in the Jewish liturgy equal to John's. E. Stauffer has gone beyond the evidence seen above and presented an interesting case for the view that John even uses the *language* of the Jewish priestly tradition.[24] Without relying on his analysis which, if it survives close scrutiny, will amount to almost conclusive proof, we remain safe in postulating that John was of priestly caste. This has some bearing on the attempt to identify him, as will be seen in Part Three.

The other indisputable indication of the evangelist's intention to produce a unified piece of work is the way in which he makes cross references. Here again a comparative table will best serve our purpose:

Jn. 1, 19. "And this is the witness of John. When the Jews of Jerusalem sent to him priests and Levites to ask him: 'Who are you?' . . ."

Jn. 5, 33. "You sent to John, and he bore witness to the truth."

Jn. 2, 11. "Jesus did this first of his signs in Cana of Galilee."

Jn. 4, 46. "He came again to Cana of Galilee where he had made the water wine." *4, 54.*

28

"This second sign, then, Jesus did when he had come from Judea to Galilee."

Jn. 3, 1–2. "There was a man of the Pharisees, by the name of Nicodemus, a prince of the Jews. This man came to him at night."

Jn. 7, 50. "Nicodemus . . . who had come to him previously . . ."

Jn. 19, 39. "Nicodemus, who first had come to him at night . . ."

Jn. 3, 14. "As Moses lifted up the serpent in the wilderness, so must the Son of Man be lifted up."

Jn. 12, 34. ". . . how do you say that the Son of Man must be lifted up?"

Jn. 5, 1–10. Jesus heals the paralytic on a Sabbath.

Jn. 7, 23. ". . . are you angry with me because I gave a man health on a Sabbath?"

Jn. 7, 33. "Jesus said to them . . . 'You will seek me but will not find me, and where I am you cannot come'."

Jn. 13, 33. "You will seek me, and as I told the Jews, 'where I am going you cannot come'."

Jn. 9, 1–7. Jesus heals the man born blind.

Jn. 10, 21. "Can a demon open blind men's eyes?" *11, 37.* "Could not he who opened the eyes of the blind man . . ."

Jn. 11, 2. "It was the Mary who anointed the Lord with perfume . . ."

Jn. 12, 3. "Mary then, taking a pound of perfume . . . anointed the feet of Jesus."

Jn. 11. Jesus raises Lazarus.

Jn. 12, 1. 9. 17. References to the fact that Jesus had raised Lazarus from the dead.

29

Jn. 11, 49–50. "One of them, Caiaphas, high priest in that year, said to them: 'You know nothing, nor do you realize that it is for your good that one man should die for the people . . .' "

Jn. 18, 14. "It was Caiaphas who had advised the Jews that it was expedient for one man to die for the people."

Jn. 13, 38. "Indeed, I tell you the cock will not crow before you have abjured me three times."

Jn. 18, 27. "Once more Peter denied it and immediately a cock crowed."

It is possible that some of these cross references could have been added by an editor, but most of them are an integral part of the contexts in which they occur (specifically, 5, 33; 7, 23; 10, 21; 11, 37; 12, 34; 13, 33; and 18, 27), in which case it is pointless to argue about the few whose omission would not matter.

III. THE PRESENT STATE OF THE MANUSCRIPT

Although the gospel bears such distinctive marks of careful planning, it also contains numerous anomalies which point to a long and unfinished process of editing. These should all be examined, moving in turn from the most obvious and least problematic examples to the most puzzling and least clear-cut.

First of all, there are the two conclusions to the gospel (Jn. 20, 30–31; 21, 25). As mentioned earlier, what is now the final chapter is generally received as an appendix added after the death of the evangelist.[25] Among the reasons for adding it was, evidently, the need felt by the

30

disciples of John to explain his death (21, 20–23). But there is very good reason for believing that the conclusion now found at 20, 30–31 was part of the appendix composed by the disciples.[26] This is of no small interest since, as we shall see, it affects the question of the evangelist's purpose.

The other conclusion (21, 25) is more troublesome. It was not in the text used by the copyist of one of our best ancient codices,[27] and several later Greek codices add "some say this [verse] is an addition." [28] On the other hand, this verse *was* known to Origen,[29] who is one of our principal witnesses to the early state of the Greek New Testament. Despite the scorn with which it is sometimes treated, it may be conjectured that this verse was in fact the evangelist's own conclusion and properly belongs at 20, 30.

Secondly, there are two rather large sections of material which appear to have been inserted in their present position by the evangelist as an afterthought. It is particularly hard to doubt this is the case of chapters 15 to 17 inclusive. At 14, 31 Jesus says to the disciples: "Rise, let us go from here," and chapter 18 begins: "Having said these things, Jesus went out with his disciples . . ." But chapters 15, 16, and 17 form a long, continuous discourse presumably given in the upper room. C. K. Barrett suggests that the material in these chapters was originally a set of eucharistic sermons subsequently edited and inserted here as alternative versions of the Lord's farewell address.[30] Lagrange had earlier proposed that this material belonged to other periods of the ministry and that 15, 1–17, for example, most naturally fell into place after the call of the first disciples. This particular hypothesis will serve us later in another respect.

The other section which appears to have been added is composed of chapters 11 and 12. R. E. Brown has argued convincingly that chapter 10 was originally followed by chapter 13.[31] There is indeed no verse in either chapter 10 or chapter 13 to support this contention—as 14, 31 does with respect to chapters 15 to 17. However, the way in which John makes the raising of Lazarus the occasion for the Sanhedrin's decision to put Jesus to death (11, 45–53; 12, 9–11)—a turn of events found only in John—and the similarity, noted by Lightfoot, between Jn. 10, 22–39 and Mk. 14, 55–64, do justify the contention. In the original form of the gospel, the charge of blasphemy laid against Jesus at 10, 33 would have explained his eventual arrest, which was already attempted at 10, 39. In any case, we must await the publication of Morton Smith's book on the recently found letter of Clement of Alexandria [32] before more can be said about the prehistory of the Lazarus episode, its position in the gospel, and John's motive for using it as he does.

Within smaller sections John seems also to have made additions, not by way of inserting new material, but by giving another, different, interpretation of what has been recounted. In chapter 6 the "bread from heaven, the bread of life" is the teaching of Jesus (6, 63), but in another sense Jesus gives his very flesh and blood as food to his disciples (6, 48–58). Similarly, in chapter 13 the foot washing is a practical example of the kind of relationship

32

which should exist among the disciples of Jesus (13, 12–17), but it is also a sacramental sign, an allusion to baptism and its effects (13, 10). In these instances John adds a new dimension to his text. Whether both interpretations were written down at the same time or one was added some time after the other cannot be ascertained, but those who have dealt with these passages see them as examples of the evangelist's protracted refining of the gospel.[33]

It might seem that a discussion of insertions and additions should include some reference to textual dislocations and interpolations, but we will not concern ourselves with these matters, for neither textual dislocations—if there are any (and this will never be settled unless the actual autograph of the gospel be discovered!)—nor interpolations (the most important of which are Jn. 5, 4 and Jn. 7, 53—8, 11) can be attributed to the evangelist.

We turn, rather, to a feature of the gospel which has not received sufficient attention from its admirers but which, once seen, bespeaks more effectively than anything else the unfinished form in which the gospel exists. This can be characterized as the disparity in literary quality between one chapter and another. "Chapter" is used here in the sense of "unit." The division of biblical books into chapters is relatively late, but the correspondence between "unit" and "chapter" is, on the whole, very close. Generally speaking, we find three types of chapters in John: those in which discourse and narrative are blended to perfection; those in which discourse (usually monologue) predominates; and those in which narrative predominates. The finest examples of the first type are chapters 7 and 9 (others are 1, 19—2,

11; 4, 3–42, and ch. 11); we find representative examples of the second type in chapters 3, 5, 8, and 10; and of the third type at 4, 43–54 and 6, 1–21, as well as in chapter 12. The first type of chapter is full of movement and dramatic intensity; the dialogue moves forward with gathering momentum, and the inevitable climactic declaration does not require a long preparatory discourse by Jesus because that has been taken care of by all the other elements in the structure of the episode. This description need not be defended, since it is acknowledged by students of the gospel that a chapter like 9 shows "consummate artistry." [34] The same cannot be said for the other types. Indeed, the theological content of chapters such as 3, 5, 8, and 10 is rich, as we shall have reason to see in the next part of this study, but John is capable of condensing and thereby of heightening the effect of the words of Jesus. We have only to contrast, as we shall, chapter 5 with chapter 9. They are both concerned with the nature of "sin," but the reader has a much clearer understanding of this from a reading of chapter 9 than from a reading of chapter 5. The long discourses in these chapters of the second type tend to ramble, and the dialogue, where it is introduced, contributes little if anything to the development of the theme. In chapter 3, for instance, Nicodemus has nothing more to say after verse 9, and in chapter 5 Jesus speaks to the Jews from verse 19 to verse 47 without their once interrupting. Chapter 3 is also remarkable for the lack of any noticeable connection between the festal background (Passover) and the discourse material. True, there is a reference to the brazen serpent (3, 14) which might be

34

considered a wilderness theme, but it is not enlarged upon at all.

But if the literary weakness of the second type of chapter is the prevalence of monologue, the weakness—always in terms of John's creative gifts—of the third type of section is the failure to develop a theme through discourse or dialogue. The cleansing of the Temple at 2, 13–22 provides a theme (2, 19–21): Jesus as the new and indestructible Temple, but the evangelist does nothing with it. This short episode, whose position here at the beginning of the gospel indicates the importance John attached to it, has also been left without any link to the liturgical setting. It is tempting to conjecture that before the evangelist decided where to situate the cleansing of the Temple in his gospel, its place was held, as Lagrange would seem to suggest, by what is now Jn. 15, 1–17.[35]

The second miracle at Cana also lacks any thematic development. A. Feuillet [36] has tried to relate it to that part of the long discourse of Jesus in the following chapter which deals with the giving of life (Jn. 5, 19–29), but there is a definite break between 4, 54 and 5, 1, and the subject matter of chapter 5, as already stated, is the nature of sin. This miracle, then, lies in the text as part of the received tradition to which John has not attached any further interpretation. He does this again with the walking on the water episode at 6, 16–21 [37] and the anointing at Bethany at 12, 1–8.[38] None of these "undeveloped" sections is without significance, of course, but they are atypically Johannine—like nuggets of gold which the evangelist had no time to refine.

35

The last of the items to be brought forth here as evidence of the unfinished state of the gospel may with equal probability be rather an indication of differing theological perspectives accepted by the evangelist, though not without an inner tension as to which expresses the truth more fully. There is in John's gospel and in the first epistle a twofold eschatology and, as will be argued in the next part of this study, a twofold Christology. Here we will confine ourselves to the problem of the two eschatologies, best seen at a glance in the juxtaposed passages constituting Jn. 5, 24–29:

Jn. 5, 24–25. "Truly I say to you that he who hears my word and believes him who sent me has eternal life, and does not come to judgment but *has passed from death to life.* Truly I say to you that the hour is coming, *indeed it is now,* when the dead will hear the voice of the Son of God, and those who have heard will live."	*Jn. 5, 27–29.* "Indeed he [the Father] has given him power to execute judgment because he is the Son of Man. Do not marvel at this, for the hour is coming in which all who are in the tombs will hear his voice and will come forth; those who have done good to a resurrection of life, those who have acted basely to a resurrection of judgment."

Verse 26, "As the Father has life in himself, so has he also given to the Son the possession of life in himself," is transitional. The differences in these passages are quite evident. The listener who is physically alive and who hears the word of Jesus, that is, accepts it, passes then and there from death to life. Until that moment of encounter with the word of Jesus men are dead, but that moment has arrived and these dead men will hear and those who receive the word will live. This is the plain meaning of the first

36

passage. In the second passage the voice of the Son of Man (as contrasted with the title "Son of God" in the earlier passage and the neutral title "Son" in the transitional verse) will, *at some undetermined future time,* be heard by those who are physically *buried* (in the tombs), and it will call them forth to judgment: bodily resurrection, which in the case of the good will carry "life" with it and, in the case of the wicked, "judgment." This last passage is, of course, representative of what may be called orthodox Pharisaic Judaism and looks forward to a life in *the Age to Come.* The first passage represents what is called "realized eschatology," and while not denying a future resurrection, stresses the possibility of entering into "eternal life" in the present age. The two ideas are juxtaposed again in chapter 11. Jesus says there to Martha: "Your brother will rise [again]," referring of course to the miracle he is about to perform; Martha, not knowing that this was his reference, says: "I know that he will rise in the resurrection on the last day," expressing here the accepted Pharisaic view. Jesus does not affirm or deny that; rather, he speaks of himself as the Resurrection and the Life and then continues: "He who believes in me, even if he die, will live," implying thereby that there is a continuing life after physical death. It is significant, however, that he does not say here: "even if he die, will rise again." He continues: "and everyone who is alive and believes in me shall not ever die." Here the emphasis is on an eternal life experienced by the living which makes physical death meaningless to them.

Other references to the "futurist" eschatology occur at

Jn. 6, 39. 40. 44. 54; 12, 48; 1 Jn. 4, 17—none of them being more than a conventional formula ("on the last day," "on the day of judgment"). The "realized" eschatology is inherent in all the gospel passages where Jesus speaks of eternal life, and that means it is to be found in almost every chapter. It appears as well in every chapter of the first epistle, with 3, 13–14 standing out as a most forceful expression of it.

These eschatologies are not contradictory, but if considered independently of one another they certainly place different emphases on life and death and have correspondingly different effects. An exclusive preoccupation with life in the "Age to Come" can have profoundly deleterious social and psychological consequences, as Marx and Freud have reminded the Christian world.[39] Moreover, although the futurist eschatology does, or should, presuppose an "eternal life" begun on earth, the realized eschatology does not *require* another "beginning" at a future date and would prescind from such a notion if it were not challenged to incorporate it because it had been received as a revealed truth.

These considerations help us to understand why John must have found it difficult to combine the two eschatologies. If he was, or rather, had been a priest, as we have concluded, and for that reason also possibly a Sadducee, there would have been a personal aspect to the problem as well.[40] Juxtaposition represents a minimal effort on his part to combine these eschatologies. Was he content with this, or are we witnessing simply the first stage of a painstaking process which time did not permit him to realize?

An interesting Latin prologue to the fourth gospel, of uncertain date [41] and of even more uncertain authority,[42] attributes to Papias the statement that the fourth gospel was given to the Church by John while he was *"adhuc in corpore constituto"*—"still possessed of a functioning body." This intriguing phrase (a crude translation of a lost Greek original) has been variously interpreted (as is anything which has come down to us from antiquity), but one not improbable meaning is that the death of the evangelist and the completion of the gospel were simultaneous events.[43] We know from the appendix to the gospel that it was *published* after his death, but, as we have also seen, there is much within the gospel to suggest that the book was not ready for publication at any time before his death. This raises one last question: What then was the motive behind the composition of a work over which the author apparently labored for so very long a time?

IV. THE PURPOSE OF THE EVANGELIST

It goes without saying that numerous answers have been given to this question. In one sense, surely, the very ancient one recorded by Clement of Alexandria remains true: John, perceiving that the "external facts" had been duly set forth in the other gospels, composed his own as a "spiritual" counterpart.[44] This withstands any criticism. Other views, ancient and modern,[45] which see in the gospel a polemic directed against this or that heretic (or heresy) tend to cancel out one another, as do most certainly the opposing

39

hypotheses about the audience for which the gospel was designed.[46] Given the time and effort expended on the composition of the work, one is easily persuaded that, as Barrett has remarked, the evangelist "wrote primarily to satisfy himself."[47] Naturally, the evangelist's conception of the work and person of Christ was no secret hidden from his listeners, and there can be little doubt that the gospel incorporates more than one preached sermon of his,[48] but the written gospel as such gives the very strong impression of being both a personal confession of faith and a monument to the divine person who commanded that faith. A monument is a work of art intended, by means of that art, to offer lasting praise. We have already had occasion to appreciate some examples of John's artistry: his effective use of details with symbolic significance, his fusion of dialogue with inset liturgical motifs,[49] and his ability to fashion a narrative which is vivid, powerful, and controlled. In these final paragraphs in our study of the formation of the gospel we must examine still other examples of Johannine art.

John can evoke a whole atmosphere together with its attendant sense perceptions by a few strikingly suggestive words. In this manner also he frequently underlines the irony of a situation. At Jn. 10, 23, after setting the scene in Jerusalem at the feast of the Dedication of the Temple (Hanukkah), the evangelist adds: "and it was winter." Is this just a pedestrian reminder that Hanukkah occurred in our month of December? From the beginning of chapter 4 the mounting hostility of the Jews towards Jesus is carefully noted. At 4, 1 Jesus becomes aware of the ill will of the Pharisees, and at 4, 44 he alludes to the lack of esteem for him encountered in Judea. In chapter 5 we learn that the Jews began now to persecute Jesus (v. 16) and even to contemplate putting him to death (v. 18). In chapter 6 it is among his own disciples that he meets with contradiction (v. 66), and it is there also that he predicts betrayal by one of the chosen Twelve. In chapter 7 an attempt is made to arrest him (v. 32), and in chapter 8 the Jews would have stoned him to death had he not escaped from their midst (v. 59). Chapter 9 reveals the intensely bitter antagonism of the Pharisees not only towards Jesus but towards anyone who spoke well of him. When we are told that "it was winter" at 10, 23, it is the climate of antipathy surrounding Jesus that we feel and the congealed hearts of his enemies that we sense. And indeed it is in this chapter during his last public appearance before the final entry into Jerusalem that the Jews make their last unsuccessful attempt to stone Jesus (vv. 31. 39).

With a similar phrase at 13, 30, John brings into focus the true nature of the deed that Judas, who had just left the Supper room, was about to perform. "And it was night," the evangelist states. The hour of the power of darkness —that darkness which figures so prominently in the gospel —had arrived, and Judas, its agent, went forth to extinguish the light of the world.[50] The tragedy and irony of this event is brought into focus a second time by John in a detail not to be found in the other gospels: "Judas, having taken a detachment of soldiers and attendants from the chief priests and Pharisees, comes there with *lanterns* and

41

torches and weapons" (Jn. 18, 3). As Hoskyns points out, this verse recalls Jn. 1, 5: "the light shines in the darkness and the darkness did not perceive it." The forces of darkness, fully equipped with lanterns and torches, approach him who is the light of the world and do not recognize him in their light, which is only darkness (vv. 4–7).[51]

At Jn. 12, 3, we read how Mary of Bethany anointed the feet of Jesus with a rare and costly perfume. The evangelist then adds: "and the house was filled with the fragrance of the perfume." There is a long exegetical tradition favoring the view that this is more than a factual comment. It may be John's poetic paraphrase of Mk. 14, 9: "wherever the gospel is preached in the whole world, what she has done will be told in memory of her." Or, as has been argued more recently, it may be an allusion to a commonplace noticed also by Polybius and mean: "thus did the pleasing aroma proclaim the presence of a king."[52] But even if this sentence were intended as no more than a statement of fact, it would be worth singling out for attention here. Pungent odors make immediate and strong impressions and create lasting associations, attractive or repellent. What John reveals to us on that level alone in this verse is his sensitive concern to associate a lavish and loving deed with an intoxicating sense experience.

The kind of sensitivity to the use of language evidenced by John leads one to suspect that he would have had a natural interest in literature as such, in literary forms and in literary styles. That he was thoroughly conversant with the sacred books of Israel has been impressively shown by others.[53] A familiarity with other Jewish literature, rabbinical and sectarian, can also be argued, though it is not necessary that the examples for this require an actual acquaintance with specific works.[54] Much has been written about his exposure to and adaptation of Gnostic thought and terminology,[55] but far too little about the indications in his gospel of an awareness of the classic literature of Greece, the plays of the great dramatists, and the dialogues of Plato. This aspect of his book has been touched upon but is generally ignored.[56] It was, perhaps, in reaction to the hasty judgment of the earlier critics that the fourth gospel was a thoroughly Hellenistic creation that further exploration of such possible evidence was inhibited. On the face of it, however, it is hard to believe that a man who was as much in touch with the various cultural currents of his world as was John,[57] could have remained ignorant of and unaffected by the rich heritage of Greece's golden age. As the Oxyrhynchus papyri show, an extraordinary range of Greek classical literature was not only available in that mere nome capital during the Roman period (and therefore in any fairly large town, to say nothing of the great cities), but much in demand as well.[58]

There are elements of *modern* drama in John, of the perennially "dramatic," as earlier passing reference to chapters 7 and 9 intimated, but if we are to speak of the gospel in terms of ancient Greek drama, it must be on the basis of roles and structure. Though it is a less obvious patterning than the liturgical one already discussed, the gospel follows quite closely, perhaps only by coincidence, the general format of classical tragedy. It has a *prologue* which focuses attention on the main theme and links together disparate elements (the Baptist and Moses with the incarnate Word), a *parados* in which the chorus sets the "emotional tone" of the drama,[59] and *episodes* separated periodically by a *stasimon,* a choral interlude in which significant comment is made on the previous action. John seems to have three of these stasima, appropriately placed near the beginning, the middle, and the end of the gospel (Jn. 3, 31–36; 12, 36–43; 19, 35–37). One might look upon "the Jews" as John's chorus, but the minor characters in the gospel—there is, of course, only one principal role—would serve as well, for both the Jews and the subordinate characters perform the functions of a chorus: to articulate Everyman's point of view, and to assist, if only by making mistakes, the advancement of the plot.[60] There is not a great deal of movement in the Greek tragedy; the emphasis is on lengthy discourse by the principals. This can also be said of a great part of the fourth gospel, though the explanation, as we have seen, may lie elsewhere than in a hypothetical Greek model.[61]

The classical chorus furthers the course of the drama in the same way that the participants in Plato's dialogues facilitate the progressive exposition of Socrates' thought, and this is why the fourth gospel is occasionally likened to the famous dialogues. Perhaps even more interesting points of comparison may be suggested. The third chapter of John contains the first lengthy discourse by Jesus, one in which the key themes of rebirth and eternal life, judgment, and the choice of light or darkness are broached, and one which is entered upon in conversation with the learned Nicodemus, a representative of Israel's most authoritative

44

religious body. Similarly, if one reads the dialogues in the order in which they are meant to be read, the first to be opened will be the *Euthyphro,* in which Socrates engages in conversation with a seer and religious expert (Euthyphro) who, it turns out, really does not comprehend religious values at all (as with Nicodemus). Though well disposed to Socrates, he is typical of the kind of person the philosopher's relentless logic has alienated.

It is in the *Apology* that Socrates describes at length his purpose in life and its consequent vicissitudes. It was his aim, he says to show those who pretended to knowledge that they were in truth ignorant, but at the cost of losing their good will and driving them ultimately to the instigation of a plot designed to crush him. Chapter 9 of the fourth gospel sums up, perhaps better than any other, John's conception of the work of Jesus,[62] and it is at the end of that chapter, in which the now irrational antipathy of the Pharisees reveals itself, that Jesus describes the purpose of his mission in terms so similar to those of Plato's Socrates. Finally, attention may be called, as indeed it has been,[63] to the rather obvious though broad parallel between the *Phaedo*—in which Socrates, just before his death, speaks at length to his friends about the virtuous life and the mystery of a life after death—and the long farewell discourse of Jesus to his friends (Jn. 15, 15) in Jn. 13—16. Allowing for the kind of striking similarities which are bound to recur in the lives of towering men of the spirit, we may yet wonder if in the selection and arrangement of *some* of his material John did not half-consciously follow this earlier model. The question assumes even more

45

pertinence if—as is almost certain in the case of chapters 13 to 17, and possible in the case of chapter 3 [64]—the present position of two thirds of the material in the gospel was due to a later revision by the evangelist.

One last query: Does John ever make any use of the content of pagan literature, that is, of its religious mythology? In a stimulating article written just over twenty years ago, the late Wilfred Knox took up the question of a "Divine Hero Christology" in the New Testament.[65] Confining himself to an examination of certain texts from Paul and the Epistle to the Hebrews, it was his view that the affinity they bore to the descriptions and panegyrics of Heracles (the archetypal "divine hero") could hardly be due to chance. Deliberate borrowing need not be postulated, he admitted, since popular philosophy could have mediated such utterances into the religious language of the synagogue or Church without betraying their ultimate origin. On the other hand, he adds, Paul may have consciously adapted appropriate texts by way of exemplifying what is said to the Athenians at Acts 17, 23: "what therefore you worship not knowing, this I preach to you." More recently, a small contribution along similar lines has suggested that John at least alludes to the widely popular figure of Heracles [66] as conqueror of Death in the language he uses to extol Jesus and the young Christian as truly Death's victors.[67] More than this cannot be said.[68] The early Church had no need of pagan cultic lore, and where it was noticed it was almost always for purposes of denigration. The occasional use of it as Christological embroidery must be viewed as an expedient exception to the rule.

46

It may seem to some that the man who could speak so disparagingly of the "lust of the eyes and the pretentiousness of life," all of which passes away (1 Jn. 2, 16–17), is hardly likely to have been the kind of dedicated gem cutter he has here been made out to be. But, on the contrary, it is only a man keenly sensitive to surface appeal who best appreciates its limits and its dangers. Moreover, the Johannine stricture on lust for the things of this world is a little epitome of the Book of Qoheleth,[69] whose author was certainly no stranger either to the cultivated Hellenistic world in which he lived [70] and wrote some of the finest poetry in the Old Testament (Eccles. 11, 7—12, 8).

Part Two:
THE MESSAGE

What Jesus Gives

Johannine thought is elusive, but this is so because it can be missed entirely if the reader does not pay the strictest attention to his parallel rephrasings, reprises, and synonyms. Even when he defines something, which is rare, the word or words employed have to be read in terms of his use or neglect of them elsewhere. Once a key idea—and there are actually few of them—has been grasped, however, we find that the evangelist is quite consistent in his exposition of it, though the alternation of imagery persists.

It is maintained here that in the gospel and first epistle there are two fundamental themes which may be stated as: 1) What Jesus gives, and 2) What Jesus takes away.

What, then, to begin, does Jesus give according to John? In the prologue the evangelist writes that to those who received him Jesus gave "the power to become children of God" (Jn. 1, 12). That is, he opened up to them the possibility of a new life in God, the exact nature of which is described in chapter 3, as we shall see. In chapter 4 Jesus tells the Samaritan woman that he gives "living water"

(v. 10), "a fountain of water welling up for eternal life" (v. 14). This is a good example of John's metaphorical language, which he uses so frequently. He reverts to this particular image in 7, 38–39, where Jesus invites all to come and drink from him as from a source of living water. In the Wisdom literature of the Old Testament this image is rather frequent (cf. Prov. 4, 20–23; Bar. 3, 12–13; Prov. 14, 27; 16, 22; 13, 14), and it always refers to teaching. There is no reason to think John has used it in a different sense since the words of Jesus are "Spirit and life" (Jn. 6, 63). The "living water" of 7, 38 is, we are told (7, 39), the "Spirit." In chapter 6 Jesus gives the bread of life (6, 27), another metaphor borrowed from Wisdom literature (cf. Prov. 9, 5; Sir. 24, 20) and again signifying teaching. Appropriately, at the end of chapter 6 Peter exclaims that Jesus has "the words of eternal life" (Jn. 6, 68). The bread which Jesus gives is also his flesh (6, 51), and there can be no doubt that John has added here, as elsewhere, a sacramental dimension to the long discourse on the bread of life. To those who have not received his word, this gift of his flesh has no utility (Jn. 6, 63), but for those who become children of God it is a pledge of mutual commitment between teacher and disciple not to be ignored (6, 53–58).

In chapter 9 Jesus says that he has come into the world "for judgment" (9, 39). He explains what is meant by that, but before examining his words, we must note the dilemma in which the ordinary reader might find himself upon hearing these words of Jesus, for at 3, 17 the Savior states: "God did not send his Son into the world to judge the world"; at 5, 22: "the Father has given the whole course of judgment to the Son" (repeated at v. 27); at 8, 16: "I judge no one," but at 8, 26: "I have many things to say and judge about you"; finally, at 12, 47: "I did not come to judge the world." The apparent contradiction vanishes if one attends to the context. Jesus has come to judge in the sense that his word and his presence are the catalysts determining how men will bring judgment upon themselves. As explained in chapter 3 (19–21), men react to the light (Jesus and his word) positively or negatively. In chapter 5 again the judgment of the individual consists in his own acceptance or rejection of the word of Jesus (v. 24). If he listens, he has eternal life; if not, he remains in death: the choice is his. In chapter 8 it is the word Jesus speaks which judges (v. 26), just as it is in chapter 12 (v. 48). Those who listen "see" (9, 39), "come to the light" (3, 21), "pass from death to life" (5, 24). In short, the judgment of Jesus is simply the opportunity his words provide for entering into "eternal life." In the middle of the gospel, at 10, 10, Jesus declares forthrightly: "I have come that they may have life and that they may have it in exceeding abundance." The "exceedingly abundant life" is of course "eternal life" (v. 28).

We find a different statement of what Jesus gives in 14, 27 and 16, 33. In these texts it is "peace." In both instances, however, the peace flows from the instruction the disciples have received, whether from the Holy Spirit (14, 26) or from Jesus himself (16, 33), and it must therefore be at least an aspect of the eternal life which comes through an acceptance of the divine word.

53

John returns to the more familiar terms at 17, 2, where Jesus affirms that the Father has given him authority over all flesh "so that he may give eternal life" to those whom the Father had given him. A few verses later this becomes "the words thou hast given me" (v. 8 and again at v. 14), which he in turn gives to the disciples.

The last reference to giving in the gospel occurs at 17, 22 in the context of a passage to be considered later. Here Jesus gives "the glory" which the Father has given him to the disciples. As we will see, this seems to refer to that love which is at the core of eternal life.

As in the Wisdom literature from which many of the phrases have been drawn, the words "eternal life," "fountain of life," "bread of life," or just simply "life," refer to a life which is lived in accordance with a teaching or to the teaching itself. For the Old Testament writers that teaching was the Law of Moses. Obviously, this cannot be the case with John, since the Law of Moses has been superseded by the "grace and truth" of Jesus Christ (Jn. 1, 17). We must then ask what the "word" of Jesus is which brings eternal life and what kind of life is being spoken of. There can certainly be no doubt that in John's mind the consequence of faith in Jesus is "life." This conviction accounts for both the gospel (Jn. 20, 31) and the first epistle (1 Jn. 5, 13).[71]

There is really only one text in the gospel which gives us an adequate explanation of the word, that is, the teaching of Jesus, that opens to man the door of eternal life; it is Jn. 3, 7–8. Other texts confirm and enlarge slightly on this one, but their importance would be overlooked were it not for the words to Nicodemus. All of them will be objects of our study.

Nicodemus, a learned Jew, an authority and, as we are surely meant to understand by his having initiated this visit, a man of sincere interest in religious matters, comes to Jesus. His opening words are gracious and respectful (Jn. 3, 2), though they say nothing of the purpose of his visit.[72] Jesus cuts through all formality and, as if in proof of what the evangelist had said three verses previously ("He knew all men"), answers the unasked question of Nicodemus: My teaching is this: "unless a man is born again, he cannot see the kingdom of God" (Jn. 3, 3). Only here and in his repetition of the statement at verse 5 does the phrase "kingdom of God" appear in this gospel. It is of course the kingdom of God which in the Synoptic gospels Jesus announces and inaugurates. It is the closest the Synoptists come to John's "eternal life," and its presence in the text here almost certainly means that John is using a well known *logion* of the Lord. This is one indication of the importance of what grows out of it for him. The reply of Nicodemus: "How can a man be born when he is old? Can he enter his mother's womb a second time and be born?", is usually taken as one of the many examples in this gospel of the naïve or sarcastic question put to Jesus by those who do not understand him (the Samaritan woman at 4, 11 perfectly exemplifies this, as do the disciples at 4, 33). But the first part of Nicodemus' reply suggests that he did indeed understand Jesus and that he is saying: "Come now, we all know you can't teach an old dog new tricks!" That, however, is precisely what the

55

learned Pharisee must accept: the possibility of a new life,
a life—given what we can take for granted about him—
which substitutes divine challenge for human assumptions.
Jesus explains: "Do not marvel that I said to you: men
must be born again." [73] This verse is important because
it shows that what follows in verse 8 is an explanation of
how it is possible for Nicodemus, or any man, to experience a new birth; or rather, it describes the simplicity of
the process: "The wind blows where it will and you hear
its sound, but you do not know from where it has come or
where it is going. So it is with everyone born of the Spirit."
As one can hear the wind, one can also "hear" the Spirit
within, but one does not know the source or the course of
the wind. Similarly, one may not fully grasp the situation
which accounts for one's sensitivity to the Spirit, or all
that will issue by following it, but the man who allows
himself to be moved by the Spirit is accepting a challenge
and in this way he experiences a new life, a rebirth.[74] Such
words spoken to a Pharisee, a representative of that group
of which Jesus says in Jn. 9, 41: "you say 'We see,' therefore your sin remains," can only mean that rebirth entails
an abandonment of all false security and an opening of
the self to new growth and new vision according as the
unpredictable voice of the Spirit within prompts. This is
the word of Jesus which *brings* eternal life, for it is only
by this kind of liberation that a man escapes death. Implied
in the words of Jesus is the conviction that Pharisaism
stifles and destroys, fashioning men who have lost com-
passion in their preoccupation with formalism (Jn. 5, 15–
17; 7, 23–24), men for whom God is far less a reality

56

than the deference they pay to one another (Jn. 5, 44), and who resort to threats, slanders, and abuse when their values are questioned (Jn. 9). Of the religious leaders of Judaism Jesus can say only that they are "thieves and robbers" whose history has been one of theft and destruction (Jn. 10, 8–10 [75]), whereas he, by contrast, has come to give life.

Two other texts in the gospel complement, in different ways, the central teaching of 3, 5–8. To the Samaritan woman Jesus disassociates true worship of the Father from the two Temple sites sacred to his people (Jn. 4, 20–24). In doing so, of course, he parts company with the literal interpreters of Is. 2, 2–3 and Zech. 14, 16–19, but the stress of his words is on the importance of worship "in spirit and truth" as distinguished from merely external cult. It is, if not a new,[76] at least a neglected attitude towards religious worship which he inculcates here. Perhaps more important is the connaturality of sorts which he posits between what is worshipped and the worshipper. John develops this idea much more fully in the first epistle. The second text is Jn. 12, 25: "Who loves his life destroys it, and who hates his life in this world safeguards it for eternal life." Jesus is of course alluding to himself here, as the previous verse indicates, but the statement is meant to apply to all men as well. Once again the teaching is directed against the cult of security, whether spiritual or physical. No one, not Jesus himself, can hope to escape the anguish of risk. That is the price of spiritual maturity. In this same context Jesus dialogues with himself on this very point: "Now my soul is tortured and what shall I say?

57

Father, save me from this hour? But it is for this that I came to this hour!" (Jn. 12, 27).

We have seen what Jesus means by "being born again." It is also clear that this is something which a man must experience here and now and not beyond the grave. His entrance into a new life is his entrance into eternal life; it is a life begun at the moment the sterile past is left behind. This is the first characteristic of eternal life as John describes it (Jn. 5, 24; 11, 26; 1 Jn. 3, 14; 5, 11–13).

We must digress momentarily to recall that John also has something to say about a life beyond the grave. The doctrine of final resurrection is given no prominence in his eschatology, as noted in Part One, and some exegetes even choose to view the references to it in the gospel as interpolations; [77] but the curious twofold eschatology of Jn. 5, 24–29, despite the problems it presents, and the evangelist's more subtle contrast of the realized and futurist perspectives in chapter 11 (which will be analyzed in Part Three) show that he accepted the idea of future resurrection, unlike some Christians who proclaimed it as an already accomplished fact (cf. 2 Tim. 2, 18).[78] Those who believed the resurrection had already taken place are more likely to have been millenarists of Jewish apocalyptic background than Gnostics whose contempt for matter might have expressed itself in some such metaphor. In accepting while not stressing a final resurrection, John distinguishes himself from both groups.

A related though distinct matter is the question of John's belief in the Second Coming. Some exegetes suggest that John has substituted the coming of the Holy

Spirit for the Parousia, [79] since apart from the one clear reference to the latter at 21, 22–23 (which, being in the so-called appendix, probably does not derive from John but from his disciples), the Parousia is not mentioned in the gospel. It is, however, taken for granted in the first epistle (1 Jn. 2, 28; 3, 2), where John also refers to the present time as "the last hour" (1 Jn. 2, 18). But just as he builds nothing on the doctrine of bodily resurrection in the gospel, so in the epistle the Second Coming has relevance only in terms of what the Christian has achieved before it occurs! "We shall be like him, for we shall see him as he is" (3, 2). The sight of the individual who has risen to the level of eternal life penetrates beyond the superficial veils of flesh and bone. There is a real parallel between 1 Jn. 3, 2 and Jn. 4, 23–24, since the idea of connaturality is common to both passages. [80]

We have determined thus far that eternal life is an abandonment of the false security which distorts and destroys any true notion of religion, an opening of the self to the promptings of the Spirit, and an experience which must begin here and now. This would be a rather threadbare description of "eternal life" if it represented all John had to say on the subject. It does not.

In both the gospel and the first epistle John gives a succinct definition of eternal life. In the gospel it occurs at the beginning of the long prayer which constitutes chapter 17: "This is eternal life, that they know thee, the only true God, and Jesus Christ whom thou hast sent" (Jn. 17, 3). This knowledge, however, is not merely something received from without, communicated by word or sight, but something welling up from within (Jn. 4, 14), for as Jesus tells the disciples a little earlier: "he who loves me will be loved by my Father, and I shall love him, and I shall reveal myself to him" (Jn. 14, 21). Again: "If anyone loves me, he will keep my word, and my Father will love him, and we shall come to him and make our dwelling with him" (Jn. 14, 23). Eternal life is primarily the reciprocal love between believer and the divine persons, a love which constitutes a way of knowing, as indeed love always does. That Jn. 17, 3 is to be read in the light of 14, 21. 23 is clear from John's restatement of the nature of eternal life in the epistle: "And we know that the Son of God has come, and has given us understanding so that we might know him who is true,[81] and we are in him who is true, in his Son Jesus Christ. This is the true God and eternal life" (1 Jn. 5, 20). Here, knowing and indwelling are juxtaposed, as they should be. The word translated as "understanding" in this text occurs only here in the Johannine writings. The earliest commentator on this epistle, Clement of Alexandria, gives it the meaning "faith" which, he continues, is to be identified with the Holy Spirit.[82] This interpretation is fully in accord with Johannine thought (cf. Jn. 14, 17. 26) and brings out even more strongly the relationship between indwelling and knowing.

But if the reciprocal knowledge-through-love between God and man is the ultimate experience of eternal life, the love of man for his brother is hardly less substantive: "By this all will know that you are my disciples, if you have love for one another" (Jn. 13, 35). John presents

60

Jesus as making this the touchstone of his teaching, in which case it must be the very fabric of eternal life, since it is eternal life which Jesus comes to give. The emphasis placed on loving one another is very marked in the gospel (13, 35–35; 15, 12–13. 17), and it literally permeates the first epistle (see also 2 Jn. 5–6). The significance of this will become clear when we enter later into a consideration of John's Christology, for it is in love, or perhaps more exactly in *loving* that the question: What is God— in himself and in Christ—meets the question of man's participation in eternal life.

It would be unthinkable to conclude this section without calling attention to the central position of Jesus in this gospel. Central not merely because he is the principal protagonist and teacher, but insofar as he illumines every page of it. The reader is, as it were, blinded by the brilliance of his image and comes away from the gospel like a man who has looked long at the sun—unable to see anything but its light. Devotion to the person of Jesus and faith in his word are crucial (Jn. 14, 1; 15, 4–6; cp. 1 Jn. 2, 23; 4, 15; 5, 12). Understandably so, for only Jesus has truly heard the Father (Jn. 8, 40), and therefore only he can explain him and lead us to him (Jn. 1, 18; 14, 6). Without faith in him we do not know where we are going (Jn. 12, 35). But further, he and the Father are one (Jn. 10, 30; 14, 9–10), and he remains forever the focal point of the divine presence in the world.[83]

What Jesus Takes Away

If what Jesus gives is eternal life, and this we have defined, we must now ask what he takes away. This the fourth gospel tells us in the very first chapter: he takes away *the sin* of the world (1, 29). In what that sin consists is not there specified, and it is our aim to discover what in fact this "sin of the world" is in the gospel. It is *one* thing which alienates the world from God: sin, not sins. What is it that underlies the sinfulness of men?

It is a curious and undoubtedly significant fact that John's references to sin in the gospel are concentrated in chapters 8 and 9. Sin is mentioned twelve times in these two chapters, as compared to eight other references scattered throughout the gospel. This suggests that here we will find the evangelist's attempt to define sin. However, the next reference to sin after 1, 29 and before chapter 8 is in chapter 5, a chapter which has been regarded by many as a sort of preliminary draft of chapter 9. An overview of the parallel structure of the two chapters will be helpful as confirmation of this surmise:

Chapter 5	Chapter 9
v. 1. Setting at the Sheep Gate.	*v. 7.* Setting near the pool of Siloam.
v. 8. Jesus cures the paralytic.	*v. 7.* Jesus cures the blind man.
v. 10. It was sabbath.	*v. 14.* It was sabbath.
v. 12. The Jews ask for information about Jesus.	*v. 17.* The Pharisees ask what the man born blind has to say about Jesus.
v. 14. The paralytic had sinned according to Jesus.	*v. 3.* The blind man had not sinned according to Jesus.
v. 18. Jesus is reviled because he broke the sabbath.	*v. 24.* Jesus is called a sinner because he breaks the sabbath (v. 16).
v. 19. Jesus affirms that the Son can do nothing of himself (so again in v. 30).	*v. 33.* If Jesus were not from God, he could do nothing.
v. 22. The Son has been given the whole course of judgment (as Son of Man, v. 27).	*v. 39.* For judgment has Jesus come into the world (Son of Man, v. 35).
v. 44. The Jews cannot believe because they are committed to honoring one another (the closed system).	*v. 41.* The Pharisees say they "see" (closed system), therefore their sin remains.
v. 45. The Jews set their hope on Moses, who will accuse them.	*v. 29.* The Pharisees call themselves disciples of Moses.

To see the way in which the evangelist repeats and reworks his teaching is not to say that he does not use actual events in the life of Jesus as his point of departure, but rather that he keeps searching for the true significance of those events.

After he had been cured and found again in the Temple by Jesus, the paralytic is cautioned: "sin no more lest something worse happen to you" (Jn. 5, 14). On the face of it this admonition seems to imply that sickness is the fruit of personal sin, a view popularly held at the time of

Jesus.[84] But precisely such a view is rejected by Jesus in this gospel in chapter 9 (v. 3, cf. above) and elsewhere in the New Testament (Lk. 13, 1–5). This immediately points to the "sin" in question as being something other than the violation of a precept. The introductory details of the story help us to determine what it is. John tells us that the man for whom Jesus performs this miracle has been ill for thirty-eight years (v. 5), and then he tells us that Jesus *knew* he had already been there a long time (v. 6). Yet Jesus asks the man: "Do you wish to become healthy?" Jesus questions the depth of the man's desire for a cure; he seems to be saying: "If you have been coming here for thirty-eight years and have not once managed to reach the waters first (cf. v. 7), you must really want your sickness." This underlying satisfaction with his lot is the man's sin. The mention of thirty-eight years, hardly an accidental or incidental circumstance, leads us further. In Deut. 2, 14 we are told that thirty-eight years elapsed between the time the Israelites left Kadeshbarnea and crossed the Zered: "in the meantime, the whole generation of soldiers had perished from the camp." Like the Israelites, the paralytic had been waiting thirty-eight years to cross over to the promised land—the promised land in his case being the deliverance offered by Jesus from Law-engendered complacency. The suspicion is that the man does not wish to be freed from the Law, and this is why Jesus asks him if he wants to be healed. He, together with all his contemporary fellow Jews, is about to "perish from the camp" because they linger on in the realm of death. This interpretation [85]

is strengthened by the likely allegorical significance of
another detail: the five porticoes of the pool (5, 2). Are
they representative of the five books of the Law? It has
been thought so from ancient times,[86] and it has been suggested that this construction—the ruins of which are vis-
ible today [87]—was designed in this way for that purpose.[88]
The paralytic, then, is surrounded by the structure of the
Law, and within its confines he cannot be healed. We
should perhaps also note that the paralytic is not placed
in the water by Jesus. On the other hand, the man born
blind in chapter 9 *is* sent to the pool of Siloam in order to
recover his sight. But the evangelist tells us at 9, 7 that the
waters of Siloam are a figure of Jesus (who is "sent" by
the Father). Does he not also here in Chapter 5 tell us that
the waters of Bethzatha are *not* salvific by alluding to the
Mosaic symbolism of the five porticoes?

There is more about sin in chapter 5. The Jews became
positively homicidal in regard to Jesus because he violated
the Sabbath (v. 18). This *to them* is sin. Jesus ironically
points out the absurdity of their position by remarking that
he does no more than what the Father does (v. 19). He
then goes on to discourse at length about his principal
mission—the giving of eternal life. It is significant, however, that this point should be introduced in the context at
hand, for it becomes part of his reply to the Jews in defense
of his cure of the paralytic. The paralytic was not restored
to physical life, yet it is implied here that he, like all for
whom Jesus has come into the world, has been raised
from death. It is the death of complacency and loveless-

ness: "You do not wish to come to me that you may have life. I do not seek human respect, but I know you, for you have no godly love in yourselves" (Jn. 5, 40–41).

The next mention of sin is at 8, 21, where Jesus tells the Jews that he is going away and that they will die "in your sin." Again the singular is used, although when Jesus repeats himself at verse 24 the plural "sins" is used.[89] At the beginning of this chapter (8, 12—it is generally agreed by all today that the story of the woman taken in adultery [7, 53—8, 11], though canonical scripture, is not an original part of this gospel) Jesus proclaims himself the Light of the world and states: "who follows me will surely not walk in the darkness, but will have the light of life." Immediately the Pharisees reject his statement: "You are witnessing to yourself; your witness is not true (Jn. 8, 13). They do not accept Jesus as a light, which means that they will continue to walk in the dark, indeed, that they prefer the dark as we have already been told at 3, 19. Their sin (sins 8, 24, "evil acts" 3, 19) is their assumption that they have the light, whereas they are in the dark; this seems certain from the fact that when Jesus repeats that they will die in their sin, he qualifies the prophecy by adding: "if you do not believe that 'I am'."

At 8, 34 Jesus again speaks of the commission of sin: "Everyone who commits sin is a slave of sin." Then, speaking to the Jews he says: "If then the Son frees you, you will be really free" (v. 36). Free of what? Free of sin. But what is their sin? Is it not their refusal to be free, their willing enslavement which is the same as their preference for the darkness? Such an interpretation is sup-

66

ported by what Jesus immediately says: "you are seeking to kill me because my word has no receptacle in you" (v. 37). The Jews have said that they were free, free sons of Abraham; Jesus tells them that they are living with an illusion. If they were really free, they would make room for him and his teaching, but they react with murderous hostility because they want to hear nothing that would challenge their cherished complacency. This is the sin of which they are guilty.

The final mention of sin in chapter 8 is at verse 46: "Which of you," Jesus asks, "finds me guilty of sin?" In the previous verse he has said: "because I speak the truth you do not believe me." After asking the question he continues: "If I speak the truth, why do you not believe me?" From this sequence it seems apparent that "sin" here means untruthfulness. This requires us to determine what in context is truth and what is falsehood. We are helped by the progress of the discourse. "He who is from God listens to the words of God," Jesus says in verse 47, continuing: "For this reason you do not listen because you are not from God." Jesus of course is from God (v. 42), but the Jews are not. They are from their father the devil, a liar and the father of falsehood (v. 44), and accordingly they do not listen. He cannot be truthful who stops his ears to the truth, from which it follows that in this passage untruthfulness, the "sin," is synonymous with not listening to the words of God.

In chapter 9 we reach as definitive an answer to the question of what "sin" is in the fourth gospel as we could hope to find. Throughout most of the chapter "sin" is used in the popular sense of the word: a violation of the Law. Even Jesus uses the word in this sense at verse 3 because he is denying what his disciples are assuming, that is, that the blind man was afflicted because he or his parents had done something (broken some commandment). At verse 16 the Pharisees make clear what constitutes Jesus a "sinner": breaking the sabbath. Accordingly, they and the man born blind (using their term without accepting their judgment) refer to Jesus as a sinner (vv. 24–25. 31). At verse 16 the Pharisees make clear what constitutes Jesus way as do the disciples at the beginning of the chapter. In verse 39, however, Jesus begins to explain what sin really is. Here, as in Jn. 3, 19–21 Jesus speaks of coming into the world to effect a judgment, and the judgment results in the distinction between those who remain in darkness or blindness and those who come to the light or sight. Those who "see," though of course they do not, at 9, 39, are to be identified with those whose deeds are evil (3, 19), and we have already found this to mean "who are arrogantly complacent." Conversely, those who "do not see"—who are not convinced of their self-sufficiency—are to be identified with those who "practice the truth" (3, 21), which accords well with the interpretation already given of being "truthful" in chapter 8. The importance of 9, 40 is paramount, since without it the whole point of the climactic apothegm in verse 41 would be missed. John tells us: "the Pharisees who were with him [Jesus] heard these statements [v. 40] and said to him: 'Are we too blind?'" As Lagrange points out,[90] these Pharisees were not part of the inquisitional group which figured so prominently in most of the chapter, but rather were just curious spectators (identifiable, perhaps, with the group in verse 16, which says: "How can a man who is a sinner perform such signs?"). They appear here, Lagrange concludes, to be more embarrassed than hostile. Consequently, what Jesus says to them in verse 41 is said to them not as hostile adversaries but as Pharisees: "If you were blind you would not have sin. As it is, you say 'we see'; your sin remains." As long as they remain convinced that they fully understand the meaning of religion—and this is proclaimed by their being Pharisees—then they condemn themselves to blindness, to darkness, to "sin."

Sin is mentioned again in chapter 15. Speaking to his disciples about what they must expect from the world, he says of those who are "of the world": "If I had not come and spoken to them they would not have sin, but now they have no excuse for their sin." And then he adds: "who hates me hates my Father also. If I had not done among them the works which no one else has done, they would not have sin, but now they have also seen yet have hated both me and my Father" (Jn. 15, 22–24). If no one comes to open the minds and hearts of the complacent, they can plead an excuse, even if in fact they would not have listened; but once such a person makes his appearance, there can no longer be any excuse for their sin. Not even the words of Jesus could induce them to listen. It is perhaps important that the evangelist has Jesus accuse them of obduracy in sin here by stating first that he came and *spoke* to no avail, and only secondarily that he also acted in such a way as to recommend him and his words,

69

again in vain. The world will not listen (in this context the world has replaced the Pharisees or the Jews who are simply types of the smug worldling; cp. 1 Jn. 2, 16, where John speaks of "the pretentiousness of life"). This passage is interesting too for the way in which it couples rejection of Jesus with hate. In this respect it is very reminiscent of Jn. 5 4–42. The closed mind drives out love.

Jesus continues in chapter 16 to describe to the disciples the lot awaiting them in the world. The Paraclete, however, will come to convict the world of its sin (v. 8), a sin which is immediately defined (v. 9) as a refusal to believe in Jesus (recalling 8, 24). Here, as elsewhere in the gospel (cp. Jn. 6, 35; 10, 26–27), not believing in Jesus is best understood as refusal to heed him.

The penultimate text regarding sin in this gospel is placed in a relatively obscure context. Speaking to Pilate, Jesus says: "You would have no authority whatsoever over me [that is, against me] if it had not been given to you from above. Accordingly, he who has betrayed me to you has the greater sin" (Jn. 19, 11). The authority Pilate has over Jesus is God-given, but in the sense that God has wished Pilate to exercise his power so that the divine plan of salvation, sealed by the voluntary death of Jesus on the cross, can be fulfilled. It was not to Pilate and his world that Jesus addressed himself (that was reserved for the future —cf. Jn. 10, 16); Pilate is representative of those who, at 15, 22, might be said to have an excuse for their "sin," for indeed Pilate has been ignorant of the very existence of Jesus (Jn. 19, 9). But the betrayers—whether it be Caiaphas, Judas, or the Pharisees in general—*were* the

70

people to whom Jesus spoke, and it was their rejection of Jesus, of which his betrayal was the culmination, which revealed their sinfulness, their refusal to listen: "You are seeking to kill me because my word has no receptacle in you" (Jn. 8, 37).

The final reference to sin in the gospel does not at first sight appear to be in line with the earlier ones as we have understood them. The text is famous. After the Resurrection Jesus appeared to the disciples, breathed on them, and said: "Receive the Holy Spirit. If you forgive the sins of any, they are forgiven; if you retain the sins of any, they are retained" (Jn. 20, 22–23). We seem to be faced with a use of the term "sins" that stands by itself. But this is not the case. Bultmann and Barrett have both seen [91] that this text is very closely related to Jn. 9, 39–41, that it is in fact merely an extension of those words of Jesus. Jesus here gives his disciples power to make a judgment, the judgment as to whether or not sin—the rejection of his word—remains (Jn. 9, 41). It is the duty of the Church to "test spirits" (1 Jn. 4, 1) and in the place of Jesus to proclaim either "Behold, you have become well" (Jn. 5, 14) or "you will die in your sin" (Jn. 8, 21).

Now we must turn to the First Epistle of John to determine whether or not the same notion of sin appears there. Immediately after his introduction John writes: "God is light and in him there is no darkness whatever. If we say that we have fellowship with him and walk about in the darkness, we lie and we are not practicing the truth. But if we walk about in the light as he is in the light, we have fellowship with one another and the blood of Jesus

71

his Son cleanses us of all sin" (1 Jn. 1, 5–7). The language here is very familiar, but the thought is somewhat convoluted. As is evident from 2, 9–11, darkness and light are metaphors for hate and love. There is no possibility of "fellowship" with God if we hate (1, 6); but if we walk in the light we have fellowship with one another, that is, we love, and consequently we are absolved of all sin. Sin, then, must be the guilt due to a lack of love. The following verse is in strict parallel with verse 6: "If we say that we do not harbor sin, we deceive ourselves and the truth is not in us." Having sin and walking in darkness are synonymous, and to walk in the darkness is to hate (2, 11). Verses 8–10 insist on the need for admitting to ourselves the existence of sin within us—our readiness to hate. The writer's words, judgments, and admonitions are all reminiscent of Jn. 3 and Jn. 9, but the content is different. His concern here is with love rather than with listening. The explanation is simple. In the gospel Jesus speaks to the unheeding world which can never love unless it first frees itself from self-love. Here John speaks to those who have in fact opened their ears and hearts, but who, being human, need to be reminded of their frailty. It is clear that he does not view inevitable failings in this regard as a betrayal of their commitment, for he assures them: "but if anyone should sin, we have an Advocate with the Father, Jesus Christ, the just; and he is expiation for our sins, and not for our sins alone, but for the whole world" (1 Jn. 2, 1–2). The perfect love of Jesus makes up for man's perpetual withholding of it. John repeats this at 2, 12.

There is a long passage concerning sin in chapter 3,

72

including a definition of the word (1 Jn. 3, 4–10). It begins: "Every one who commits sin actually practices lawlessness; indeed sin is lawlessness." Is John expressing here the view upheld by the Pharisees in the gospel—that violation of the Law is the essence of sin? This important text has been studied in the greatest detail by I. De La Potterie,[92] and his conclusions have met with wide approval. According to De La Potterie, "lawlessness" (*"anomia"* in Greek) here must be understood as a state of opposition to the work of God, especially as it is revealed to us by his Messiah. It is commitment to the demonic. The word (its Semitic equivalents) figures prominently in Jewish apocalyptic literature and always has this meaning. This interpretation is confirmed by what John says at verse 8: "who commits sin is of the devil, for the devil has sinned from the beginning"—words that echo strongly the accusation of Jesus in Jn. 8, 41. 44: "You do the works of your father. You are from your father, the devil. He was a murderer from the beginning." The obvious parallel between these texts suggests that the comparison be pursued in the verses which follow each of them:

1 Jn. 3, 9: Whoever is born of God does not commit sin, because the seed of God abides in him and he cannot sin since he is born of God. Thus are the children of God and the children of the devil revealed.

Jn. 8, 46–47: Who is of God listens to the words of God. Accordingly, you do not listen because you are not of God.

The thought is the same in both passages. To sin is to close the ears to the words of God and thereby to oppose him.

But in the epistle John quickly passes from a discussion of sin to a consideration of love (1 Jn. 3, 11–24). The transitional verse is 10: "whoever does not practice righteousness is not of God, nor he who does not love his brother" (cp. v. 15). Hate is, as it were, the dynamic aspect of not listening, and of course we have already seen that hate resulted in the betrayal of Jesus (Jn. 8, 37. 40; 15, 18. 20. 24).

At 4, 10 there is another reference to "sins" which requires no comment since it is merely a repetition of 2, 2. But the final remarks of John about sin in this epistle are very instructive. He takes it for granted that Christians will see one another committing sin (5, 16), but he is very careful to describe their sins as not "deathward" (*ou pros thanaton* or *mê pros thanaton*). He continues: "There is deathward sin. I do not say that one should pray for that. All wrongdoing (*adikia* here, not *anomia*) is sin, yet there is sin which is not deathward" (1 Jn. 5, 16–17). It is not difficult to determine what the deathward sin is; we have only to recall Jn. 5, 25 and 1 Jn. 3, 14. Whoever does not open himself to the word of God and thereby dries up the wellspring of love within himself commits the sin for which John does not recommend prayer. It must be remembered that in the gospel John records Jesus as saying: "I do not pray for the world" (Jn. 17, 9). The world, in the sense intended there, is a world that has hated without cause (Jn. 15, 25), a world which embraces darkness out of preference (Jn. 3, 19). The saving word of Jesus cannot affect it, neither can the prayer of the faithful. As E. Käsemann has noted,[93] John can be icy at times. He was not a sentimentalist but a realist.

In conclusion we may say that sin, the sin from which those who listen to the word of Jesus are absolved, is first of all a false and corroding sense of self-sufficiency—which precludes the operation of grace—, and secondly but consequently, a failure to love. The sin which dooms to death is persistent refusal to examine one's presuppositions, to continue saying "we see."

Who Jesus Is

But who, for John, is Jesus? This gospel is replete with
titles given to Jesus or used by Jesus of himself: "Word,"
"Light," "Only-Begotten," "Lamb of God," "Messiah,"
"King of Israel," "Son of God," "Son of Man," "Savior of
the World," "Way," "Truth," "Life," "Resurrection,"
"Bread of Life," "Good Shepherd," "True Vine," and
simply, "I am." Most of these designations are obviously
drawn from Israel's religious literature; three or four of
them, though not alien to Old Testament usage, are more
easily recognized as Hellenistic ("Word," "Light," "Savior
of the World," and perhaps, as John uses it, "Truth").
But how much, in fact, do such titles really tell us about
Jesus? As "Lamb of God" (that is, the "Servant of the
Lord" of Is. 53, 7), "Messiah," "King of Israel," and
"Good Shepherd," he is the fulfillment of Israel's hope
for a redeeming—but not necessarily more than human—
figure (cf. Jn. 5, 39). Read in context, such designations
as "Light," "Way," Truth," "Life" (and "Bread of Life"),
"Door," "True Vine," present him as the means by which

mankind may attain eternal life, the nature of which has already been discussed. He has come to bring light, life and truth, that is, to open men's eyes and hearts so that they may live in a new way (Jn. 3, 13). Consequently, his very words are "spirit and life" (Jn. 6, 63), and to reject them is to reject Jesus totally (Jn. 8, 37); he is what he does, and that is to speak "God's words" (Jn. 3, 34). As will be seen later, it is as the incarnation of divine teaching that he is designated "Word" in the prologue to the gospel. In this way also the acclamation of the Samaritans, "This man is truly the Savior of the world" (Jn. 4, 42), should probably be understood, inasmuch as it springs from their having *heard* Jesus. All these titles then support Bultmann's contention that the Jesus of the fourth gospel is merely the Revealer without our knowing more about him. But we are left with the titles "Son of God" (or "Only-Begotten Son" or "Son of the Father"), "Son of Man," and the declaration "I am" (or, as it may be translated, "I am He"). These do, in fact, go far beyond the other titles listed in telling us who Jesus was for the evangelist, but what they tell us is not, as some maintain, all of a piece.[94] Rather, the ways in which John attempts to understand the mystery of the person of Jesus appear to be two, one utilizing the Son of Man figure and the "I am" motif and reflecting a primitive, Jewish-inspired, apocalyptic Christology; the other, it will be suggested, drawing on a source hitherto unidentified and representing the evangelist's mature understanding of the Godhead and of Jesus as identifiable with it. If Johannine Christology

77

were indeed all of a piece, we should have to admit that Käsemann's view or something very like it was the correct one.[95]

I. THE SON OF MAN CHRISTOLOGY

Initially leaving aside any consideration of relevant texts in the prologue and introduction to the gospel, and moving immediately to chapter 3, we find the Son of Man described there as *ascending to* and *descending from* heaven. It has been noted that Jesus speaks here in terms altogether like those used by the author of Baruch to describe divine Wisdom's arrival in Israel (Bar. 3, 29–38), and there can be little doubt that the figure of a Son of Man who has his normal dwelling in the sphere of the divine owes much to the descriptions of personified Wisdom in the Sapiential literature of the Old Testament.[96] The verbs "ascend" and "descend" used in Jn. 3, 13 constitute the strongest evidence for a doctrine of pre-existence —not, it is important to note, the pre-existence of the eternal Word, but of the apparently created Son of Man who is distinct from God.[97] Other terms, such as "coming from above" (3, 31) or "coming from heaven" (3, 31), "from above" (8, 23) or "come from God" (8, 42) are, in every instance, contrasted with parallel statements made to the Jews who are "from the earth" (3, 31), "from below" (8, 23), "from this world" (8, 23), or "from your father the devil" (8, 44). Since it is perfectly clear that the descriptions given of the Jews are more

78

moral than physical in character, the "heavenly" status of Jesus in these passages can and probably should be understood in terms of his relationship to the Father and not to any physical point of departure. Nevertheless, the terminology *is* vertical and, in characteristic fashion, John may have in mind the Gnostic use of such words as well as his own. For the Gnostic the human and earthly condition are literally demonic products.

In chapter 6, where Jesus describes himself as the "Bread of Life," "ascend" is used once (v. 62) and "descend" repeatedly (vv. 33. 37. 41. 42. 50. 51), and it is significant that in this chapter where the vertical language is so pervasive, Jesus three times refers to himself as the "Son of Man" (vv. 27. 53. 62). Further, in chapter 8, where Jesus talks of himself as "from above" and "not from this world" (v. 23), it is as Son of Man that he speaks (v. 28). Similarly, in chapter 9, where Jesus asks the man born blind if he believes in the Son of Man—who is himself—he immediately proceeds to characterize himself further as one who has "come into this world" (v. 39), an *automotive* phrase frequent in John and, though the difference be only nuanced, different nonetheless from the equally frequent "sent" (by the Father). In chapter 12 the title "Son of Man" occurs three times. Jesus speaks of the arrival of the hour in which the Son of Man is to be glorified (v. 23), and the Jews, in response to his statement that the Son of Man is to be lifted up, ask: "How is it you say that the Son of Man ought to be lifted up? Who is this Son of Man?" (v. 34). We have no explicit reference here to coming down from or going up to heaven, but the

close relationship between 12, 32–34 and 3, 14 is un-
deniable; in fact it is almost as though the Jews in 12, 34
were responding to the words of Jesus in 3, 13–15 rather
than to his statement in 12, 32 which makes no mention
of the "Son of Man." Furthermore, the reference to glorification at 12, 23 ties this passage to two of the strongest
texts representative of a doctrine of pre-existence: 17, 5.
24. For this reason, the last of the Son of Man texts (save
5, 27, which will be considered later): "Now has the Son
of Man been glorified, and God has been glorified in him"
(13, 31–32), also carries with it the overtone of heavenly
pre-existence.

The context of 12, 23–33 also requires us at this point
to raise the question of the "I am" statements of Jesus in
this gospel. At 12, 23 Jesus says: "The hour has come in
which the Son of Man is to be glorified," and at verse 28,
again in terms of this hour: "Father, glorify thy Name."
There is a correlation between the Son of Man and the
Name of the Father (and "I am he" was used as an equiva-
lent of "Yahweh" in both the sacred readings and the liturgy [98]). Ethiopian Enoch tells us that the Son of Man
was named before the creation of the world and that "in
his Name" the holy and righteous are saved (xlviii). If
the just are saved in the name of the Son of Man, is it not
because, like the Angel of the Lord, the divine Name is in
him? Of the Angel of Yahweh we read: "Do not rebel
against him, for he will not forgive your sin. My Name is
in him" (Ex. 23, 21). In identifying the Son of Man and
the divine Name, John or his source merely anticipates
what Jewish speculation was to do with Metatron, a me-

80

diating figure in whom all the earlier apocalyptic characterizations of a messiah-judge were summed up.[99] In short, Jesus uses the theophanic "I am" insofar as he is the Son of Man, and in support of this view is the fact that of the four instances in which "I am" cannot simply mean "it is I," but must have the force of "I am He, Yahweh," three occur in chapter 8, where this correlation between the Son of Man and the divine Name is made explicitly by Jesus: "When you lift up the Son of Man, then you will know that I am" (v. 28). This statement in 8, 28 should be regarded as a close parallel to 12, 23. 28 already examined. The fourth instance, 13, 19 (by reason of his having predicted his betrayal, the disciples will know that he is "I am"), is parallel to 6, 64, where as the Son of Man Jesus predicts his betrayal.

Accordingly, it is argued here that in this gospel Jesus, as the Son of Man, is a pre-existent heavenly being who comes down from and goes up to the Father, a being who comes into the world, who shared the Father's glory before the creation of the world, and who bears the Father's Name.[100] This Christology may be characterized as primitive, employing language that is largely mythological (apocalyptic) and obviously dependent upon the later (intertestamental) Jewish embellishments of the Son of Man figure. It represents a tentative effort to understand the mystery of the person of Jesus and an early stage in the composition of this gospel or, perhaps more correctly, an early source which the evangelist was reluctant to jettison entirely.[101] This Christology corresponds to the early, futurist, and strongly Jewish eschatology which we find here and there—but only, as it were, incidentally—in John. As is recognized, the two eschatologies, realized and futurist, are juxtaposed in chapter 5 (vv. 24–29), and it is much to our purpose to note that the one instance in this gospel where the title "Son of Man" is used independently of terminology denoting or alluding to pre-existence, that is, at 5, 27, it is nevertheless tied, as Brown and Boismard note, to the futurist type of eschatology and, accordingly, to the same layer of conceptualization to which the apocalyptic Son of Man belongs.[102] Boismard sees the Christology of Jn. 5, 26–30 as being in the same vein as that of the Synoptics precisely because Jesus is presented here as essentially the Son of Man announced by the prophet Daniel, but, he continues, the Christology of Jn. 5, 19–25 is quite different, based as it is on the "Father-Son" parallelism.[103]

As Boismard has rightly perceived, there are two Christologies in this gospel, just as there are two long-recognized eschatologies. The character of this second Christology has not been adequately developed, and no pretense is made here of fulfilling that need, but certain points can be made which others may find worth following up.

As noted, the two types of eschatology are juxtaposed in chapter 5 and, as we have also seen earlier, there are several other examples of parallel texts representing different perspectives in this gospel. The two incidents of a stoning of Jesus in this gospel, the one at 8, 59 and the other at 10, 31, appear to furnish us with another doublet, this time illustrative of the two Christologies. Here we are indeed dealing with distinct chapters rather than with the kind of parallel passages juxtaposed within the same chapter elsewhere. However, as others have recognized, there is a good example of the kind of parallelism posited here in chapters 5 and 9; chapter 9 gives us a revised, much improved version of chapter 5.[104] So chapter 10 seems to be a revision of chapter 8. It is instructive to note the precise parallels:

Chapter 8	Chapter 10
v. 17f. The witness of himself and the Father to Jesus.	*v. 25*. The witness of his works to Jesus.
v. 20. Jesus is teaching in the Temple.	*v. 22*. Jesus is teaching in the Temple.
vv. 20–22. Jesus will "go away," and the Jews ask. "Will he kill himself?"	*vv. 11. 15–18*. Jesus will freely lay down his life.
v. 25. The Jews ask: "Who are you?"	*v. 24*. The Jews demand that he tell them who he is.
vv. 27. 43. The Jews do not understand him.	*v. 6*. The Jews do not understand him.
v. 48. He is accused of having a demon.	*v. 20*. He is accused of having a demon.
v. 51. The word of Jesus gives eternal life.	*v. 28*. Jesus gives eternal life.
v. 59. The Jews pick up stones to kill him for blasphemy.	*v. 31*. The Jews pick up stones to kill him for blasphemy.

But whereas chapter 8 abounds in vertical language and references to glorification, and presents Jesus as the Son of Man using the "I am" formula of himself, chapter 10 avoids all vertical language and all mention of the Son of Man or of the divine Name. Others, false shepherds, have come before Jesus to steal and to kill and to destroy. He comes to bring Life. But he does not come *into* the world, he is *sent* by the Father (vv. 10. 36). He and the Father

are one because the Father is in him and he is in the Father
(vv. 30. 38). The language of Jesus in this chapter follows
closely (or is followed closely by) that used in the Supper
discourse at 14, 10–11 consequent upon the statement
there: "He who has seen me has seen the Father." This
may be called horizontal language and it stands in
marked contrast to the statement made at 6, 46: "Not that
anyone has seen the Father except him who is from God;
he has seen the Father."

The apparent difficulty in the way of accepting this
supposed twofold Christology in John [105] arises from the
frequent melding of vertical and horizontal language. The
two kinds of self-description used by the Jesus of the
fourth gospel are sometimes woven together so closely
that it is hard to believe they represent distinct stages in
the development of the evangelist's thought. For example,
in 8, 14 Jesus says, vertically: "I know where I have come
from and where I am going"; at 8, 19, horizontally: "If
you knew me, you would know my Father also"; but
then, again vertically: "You are from below; I am from
above" (v. 23). This difficulty is met if, as suggested, we
posit the evangelist's unwillingness to abandon a primitive Christology he had received. Chapter 8, then, can be
viewed as an earlier piece of work inasmuch as the received Christology is dominant, although the evangelist's
own developing theology emerges occasionally. In chapter
10, on the other hand, the received Christology has been
left aside. But there are examples of the juxtaposition of
the Christologies in the gospel, and they provide us with
an insight into the way in which the evangelist kept

revising the primitive teaching in his own mind. In 17, 20–26, for instance, we have two prayers. In the first prayer (vv. 20–23) Jesus expresses the wish that all may be one as he and the Father are one. This unity will demonstrate to the world that Jesus has been sent by the Father. Jesus accordingly gives to the disciples his glory, which appears to be the Father's love, since this is what the world will ultimately realize about the disciples: that they are loved as Jesus is loved. In the second prayer (vv. 24–26) Jesus expresses the wish that the disciples be *with* him, not *in* him, so that they may see the glory which Jesus has had since before the creation of the world. Here "glory" appears to be a kind of aura, and it is not said that it has been given to the disciples. What Jesus makes known to the disciples is the *Name* of the Father, and this work of his will elicit for them the love which the Father bears for Jesus and will serve to incorporate the disciples with him.

The differences in the midst of so much deceptively similar phraseology are not unimportant. The thrust of the first passage is that Jesus, confident of his utterly intimate union with the Father, draws into that oneness those who believe him, and the bond creating the total union is Love. In the second text Jesus' concern is that the disciples remain in his presence (in heaven?) so that they may see his privileged position alongside the Father whose Name he made known to them once he had come into the world. Through knowledge of the Father's Name as imparted to them by Jesus, the disciples will win the Father's love and Jesus will enter into communion with them. In a word, the difference, it seems, is between a Jesus who says: "He who

85

sees me sees the Father," and a Jesus who says: "Not that anyone has seen the Father, except him who is from God."

II. JOHN'S DEVELOPED THEOLOGY IN RELATION
TO GNOSTIC AND BUDDHIST THOUGHT

In his first epistle John reaffirms that "no one has ever seen God," but then he continues: "if we love one another, God abides in us" (1 Jn. 4, 12). One experiences God, knows in fact what God is, in loving (1 Jn. 4, 7). The man who loves is "born of God," "abides in God" as God "abides in him" because, ultimately, "God is Love" (1 Jn. 4, 7–8. 16). For us to love is to *extend* ("fulfill," "perfect") the very nature of God (1 Jn. 4, 12; cp. Paul's different but comparable statements at 1 Cor. 15, 28 and Col. 1, 24), and this is why the Christian can be said both to become God for his neighbor,[106] and to behold God in his neighbor.[107] For the same reason, the believer *already* possesses eternal life (1 Jn. 5, 13) because he is living love (1 Jn. 3, 14), which is the same as living as God. No one, however, has loved more perfectly than Jesus (Jn. 13, 1; 15, 13), which makes him alone *(monogenês)* the interpreter of the Father (Jn. 1, 18) and reveals him as the focal point of God's presence in the world (Jn. 1, 51, a text yet to be considered).

This, it may be allowed, is how John resolved the Christological problem for himself, and it is apparent that such a

Christology is also a theology of bold, even daring lines. God is not confined to a different sphere of reality from which the Son of Man has literally made a descent. He is present everywhere, focally in the person of Jesus Christ [108] but experientially—and diffusively—to all who, in response to the command of Jesus, learn to love. His presence is realized through connaturality, that is, by *doing* what he *is*. Man can achieve this by being born again, "from above" (Jn. 3, 7–8), by rendering the soil of his heart fertile so that the seed of God may take root in him (1 Jn. 3, 9), and the seed of God is godly love (Jn. 5, 42). Man can also reject divine life because he can refuse to love (cf. Jn. 5, 38; 8, 37). There is, therefore, nothing intrinsically divine about him, but he can rise to the divine level, for love assimilates him to God (1 Jn. 4, 17). Clement of Alexandria, who stands so close in time to the composition of the Johannine writings, tells us that the soul is not naturally incorruptible but achieves incorruptibility through faith, goodness, and understanding, which come to it by God's grace.[109] In this he echoes John, for whom "he who does not love remains in death" (1 Jn. 3, 14).

The "ethical" color of John's theology shows how wide an abyss exists between it and Gnostic thought. In both John and Gnosticism those who are saved are saved because they have learned the truth, but the truth for the Gnostic is knowledge of the self as divine, while for John the truth is "walking in love" (2 Jn. 4–6). In both systems, again, some are saved and some are damned, but the eternally lost of Gnostic belief are those who lack constitutionally the divine nature (the *"hylikoi"*), whereas for John the "dead" are those who spurn what is within their grasp.

At the same time that Gnosticism was beginning to acquire a recognizable form in the Mediterranean world, Mahayana Buddhism was developing in India. The two religions share certain basic premises (probably because of conscious reciprocal influence at this early stage in their histories [110]). Both maintain that the essence of redeemable man is the divine nature itself ("Buddha nature" for the Mahayanist), and both postulate that the realization of this truth—which is the same as salvation—can come through knowledge alone. But there are important differences. Authentic Mahayana Buddhism does not distinguish, as Gnosticism does, between those who are essentially redeemable and those who are not.[111] Nor does it conceive of the absolute ("Wisdom," *"Prajna"*) as a *thing;* it is an activity. Buddhahood can be defined as the very act of knowing: "just the Buddha is enlightenment, just enlightenment is the Buddha." [112] And although whoever wishes to seek for the Buddha is told to seek for the true self (the only reality related to the illusion of individuality), the identity of this "real" self and the Absolute is on the level of *doing* because, of course, Reality *is* Knowing. Furthermore, the realization of who he really is, for the Gnostic, is merely the prerequisite for a journey out of this world; for the Mahayanist the realization is Nirvana.

With respect to these differences between Gnosticism and Mahayana Buddhism, John's thought is more Buddhist than Gnostic. When he wishes to *define* God (as distinguished from his references to him, which are traditional and personalist), he employs words which denote acts or dispositions rather than a static entity. God is Spirit (Jn. 4, 24), but Spirit is an attitude (Jn. 4, 24), a disposition (Jn. 3, 8), an understanding (Jn. 6, 63); God is Light (1 Jn. 1, 5), but Light is nothing other than Love (1 Jn. 2, 10–11), about which so much is said in the first epistle; or it is integrity, "doing the truth" (Jn. 3, 20–21). Such a concept of the Divine (the Absolute) does not appear elsewhere in the Old or New Testaments, or in the inter-testamental literature, or in the Hellenistic mystery religions. Further, John's doctrine of divine indwelling (the texts are numerous but cf. especially Jn. 14, 7; 1 Jn. 4, 4. 15–16) is analogous to the Buddhist concept of Buddha nature inasmuch as the divine indwelling constitutes, as it were, a form of knowing within us.[113] Finally, his teaching that the Christian has already passed from death to life (Jn. 5, 24; 1 Jn. 3, 14) is close to the Mahayanist view of the exercise of "wisdom" as identical with the state of Nirvana. "Just the path is enlightenment," the Buddha teaches his disciple in the *Prajnaparamita,* to which the disciple replies: "If that is so, then a Bodhisattva has *already* attained enlightenment." [114]

Thus what is suggested here is that the evangelist was aware of Mahayana Buddhist doctrine—something in no way unlikely [115]—and found its way of talking about the Absolute and man's relation to it most suitable for the articulation of his own religious faith and experience. For him, however, the Absolute is not the impassive Wisdom of the Mahayana but the creative and redemptive power of

Love which, considered by itself, may properly be conceived of humanly as the Father. Correlatively, John's "eternal life" is not the Mahayanist's intuitive perception of all forms (constructions of the physical or ideal order) as "empty," that is, devoid of any self-sufficient independent reality,[116] but a radical openness to others whereby the Christian becomes *mimêtês Theou*.[117]

Barrett has said that John used Gnostic terminology because he found real theological appropriateness in the words and a content behind them that was both too near and too far from the truth to be ignored. In using a Gnostic vocabulary, however, he gave a Christianized—which often meant inverted—meaning to it.[118] This can be applied as well to the present suggestion that the evangelist also made use of Mahayana Buddhist concepts. That he did so explains perhaps what others have characterized as the "unusually complex" setting of the gospel,[119] or the singularity of John "not only in the ancient world but also in the primitive Church," [120] or the voice of John, distinct from the rest of primitive Christianity, whose "historical place" we cannot exactly locate.[121]

To complete this analysis of Johannine Christology we must return now to the prologue and introduction to the gospel. The problems raised by the prologue are well known to all. We do not know if it was an original creation of the evangelist or a hymn which he adapted to serve as a preface to his work. Neither do we know whether it inspired the gospel or merely summed it up. A case can be made for and against any one of these possibilities. Consequently, we cannot say whether the prologue in its present state reflects or represents a late or an early stage of the evangelist's thought; we can only assume that at one point or another he found it expressive of his theology. Nevertheless, it cannot be ignored since it ostensibly teaches a doctrine of pre-existence. The pre-existence, however, is of the Logos, the eternal Word or Wisdom of God, not of the "Son of Man" or any other mortal form. The aim of the prologue is to contrast Jesus and Moses, and thereby to contrast the Law and the teaching of Jesus. That Wisdom which Sirach identifies with the Law of Moses (Sir. 24, 23) is also said by him in the same passage to have "pitched its tent in Israel" (Sir. 24, 8). In John's prologue the Word also pitches its tent but by assuming corporeal, not written form. The concern of the prologue, then, is to affirm that a person, Jesus Christ, has supplanted a book, the Torah of Moses.[122] The prologue surely implies that the Law was an imperfect grasp of eternal Wisdom, for it did not communicate the Grace and Truth brought by Jesus Christ (Jn. 1, 17), and for this reason only Jesus can explain the Father. Clearly, there is nothing in the prologue inconsonant with what has been termed here the evangelist's more mature Christology.

The verbs of ascending and descending first appear together in this gospel at 1, 51, just before the last section of the introduction (the first miracle at Cana, 2, 1–11). Jesus tells Nathanael that he will see heaven laid open and the angels of God ascending and descending on the Son of Man. Much has been written as to whether or not John depends here on rabbinical commentaries on Gen.

91

28, 12, in which the angels ascend and descend on Jacob
rather than on the ladder. This is largely irrelevant. The
point is that Jacob's dream was a theophany: in it heaven
opened and the angels appeared and Yahweh stood beside
him. What Jesus is telling Nathanael is that, like Jacob
(to whom Nathanael has in fact been likened and found
superior in verse 47), he will behold God, but in the person of Jesus. As Brown concludes after reviewing all the
interpretations, the promised vision means that Jesus has
become the *locus* of divine glory.[123] This text, then, properly
belongs with those in which reference is made to seeing
God in Jesus. What must interest us is that only here has
John made use of the vertical terminology and of the Son
of Man figure with what appears to be a deliberate inver-
sion of their connotations elsewhere: the Son of Man does
not ascend or descend here; he is the *focus* of such movements. Consequently, in terms of the hypothesis of an
evolving Christology, this last text to be considered[124] must
be classified as later than all the other Son of Man passages
and evidence that for the evangelist the title "Son of Man"
could and should be freed of its apocalyptic associations.

Part Three:
THE EVANGELIST AND HIS FORMATION

The Evangelist: What the Gospel and the Epistles Tell Us

We now know that the fourth gospel was certainly in circulation during the first half of the second century, but the first formal ascription of it to "John" occurs in the writings of Theophilus of Antioch,[125] which may be dated between 170–183 A.D. Nevertheless, the bishop of Antioch does this in so off-handed a way as to make it evident that both he and his readers took this ascription very much for granted. Accordingly, we must conclude that the gospel was known as "John's" for at least a generation before their time, which brings us back to the period of its earliest verifiable appearance in Egypt and permits us to assume that its author was in fact a John. Who that John was is a question which, until modern times, it had been assumed Irenaeus (bishop of Lyons and a slightly younger contemporary of Theophilus of Antioch) had clearly answered. But before taking up the tangled web of external testimony regarding the authorship of the gospel, let us determine what the Johannine writings themselves tell us about John.

95

One thing we have already accepted: the likelihood that John had been a priest or Levite. To the reasons given in Part One, others may be added here. (1) The presence in the gospel of material peculiar to John and best attributed to a source in close contact with the ruling coterie of Jews and Romans: Jn. 11, 47–51, the account of the meeting of the Sanhedrin at which Caiaphas proposes that one man die to placate the Romans, a passage which Dodd traces to a Jewish-Christian circle in which the words of the high priest, irrespective of his personal worthiness, could truly be regarded as prophetic; [126] and Jn. 18, 12–24. 33–38 and 19, 9–11, the interrogations of Jesus by Annas (former high priest and father-in-law of Caiaphas) and Pilate (inside the Pretorium). (2) The role played in the gospel by individuals who belonged to the Jewish aristocracy. In Chapter 18 Peter is accompanied by an unnamed disciple who was known by, perhaps related to, the high priest (18, 16). This person (we shall not attempt to identify him) was surely the source of the information given about the unofficial examination by Annas. Nicodemus, the member of the Sanhedrin who comes to Jesus by night in chapter 3 and reappears at 7, 50–52 and 19, 39, is another such individual. He is indeed a "type" figure when introduced to us, but it is hard to believe the evangelist invented him. With the reference to the utterly extravagant quantity of myrrh and aloes brought by Nicodemus to the sepulcher,[127] John points at 19, 39 quite unmistakably to the noble and extremely wealthy Jerusalem family in which the name Nicodemus was current.[128] (3) The suspicion, first voiced by F. C.

Burkitt more than half a century ago, that John did not believe in the doctrine of future resurrection "apart from his Christianity." [129] Passing reference was made to this earlier in the context of our consideration of the evangelist's twofold eschatology. As noted there, John's references to "the last day" are very few in comparison with his extended presentation of a "realized eschatology," and they are very stereotyped. But the tone of chapter 11 lends the strongest support to Burkitt's suspicion. To repeat what was said previously, Martha's very precise confession of faith in bodily resurrection at the last day (Jn. 11, 24) is really ignored by Jesus. She has missed the significance of his teaching. Resurrection and eternal life are present in him, in his word (Jn. 5, 24; cp. 11, 25–26). For the believer there is no "then" without a "now," and because of what happens "now" the importance of what *will* happen "then"—for it is not denied—is greatly reduced. The concern of the evangelist to stress this, and surely to stress what he understood to be an integral part of the teaching of Jesus [130] *not* stressed otherwise, does suggest an underlying personal indifference on his part to the Pharisaic doctrine. He accepts it now because it is accepted by Jesus, who puts it in a new perspective for him. If this view of John's attitude towards bodily resurrection is correct, and if he was a Jew, then he had belonged to the priestly party of Sadducees who "say that there is no resurrection" (Acts 23, 8).

These considerations are merely corroborative of the deduction that John was a priest, since only the last would necessarily represent his own experience, but the first two items also present us with what was at least a *special* source for him.

The language of the gospel (its style rather than its terminology) and the epistles provide us with further information about John. He writes in a Greek which is simple, quite grammatical, and at times even very idiomatic.[131] The theory propounded by Burney and Torrey in the twenties [132] that the fourth gospel is a translation of an Aramaic original was never generally accepted, but it did call attention to the over-all Semitic flavor of John's Greek, the kind of phrasing which, while remaining correct Greek, betrays the mind of someone who was accustomed to thinking in Aramaic.[133] A simple example will suffice. The phrases "to walk," "to walk in the light," "to walk in the darkness," "to walk in the truth" (Jn. 8, 12; 1 Jn. 1, 6. 7; 2, 6. 11; 2 Jn. 4, 6; 3 Jn. 3. 4) always have a moral connotation and are not to be found in this sense in Greek literature but owe their origin to the Old Testament (cf. Is. 38, 3 as a good illustration). We find this usage frequently in Paul as well (and see Mk. 7, 5). Paul was born a Jew of the Diaspora for whom the first language would have been Greek, but he was educated and brought up in Jerusalem (Acts 22, 1–3). John too must have been a Palestinian Jew whose native tongue was Aramaic. This is the second conclusion we arrive at on the basis of his writings.

Can we localize his origins more specifically? Not with the same degree of assurance, but certainly the evangelist's preoccupation with the Judean ministry of Jesus (in the whole gospel we find Jesus outside of Judea only at 2, 1–12; 4; 6; 11, 54? and in the appendix), his singular preference for regarding Jesus himself as properly a Judean (Jn. 4, 44) though he knows the Lord's home was Nazareth (Jn. 1, 45–46; 7, 3. 41. 52), and his rather detailed knowledge of the topography of Jerusalem (which could, of course, have been supplied to him), count for something. To put it minimally, there is more in the gospel to indicate that the author was Judean rather than Galilean.

At 19, 35 there is an unquestionable appeal to eye-witness testimony: "He who has seen [the flow of blood and water from the side of Jesus] has testified, and his testimony is true." Is the evangelist speaking of himself here or of someone else? The verse continues: "and this one knows that he speaks the truth so that you too may believe." This additional statement has given rise to many difficulties. The word *"ekeinos," "this one,"* is capable of several meanings: it may refer to the witness just mentioned, or to Jesus, to some other unnamed corroborator, or to a group.[134] The sentence is so very like 21, 24 that one suspects it was inserted by the final editor(s) of the gospel responsible as well for the appendix. In this case the first part of the verse *would* constitute evidence that the evangelist was a witness of the crucifixion. Schnackenburg warns against pressing this argument,[135] but it is hard to escape its force since the editor(s) of the gospel also identifies the evangelist with "the disciple whom Jesus loved" at 21, 20–24. Who that disciple may have been merges with the question: Who was John?

1 Jn. 1, 1 also appears to guarantee that the writer of the epistle had heard, seen, and touched the incarnate Word, but the force of the language is weakened, if not

destroyed, if this opening verse of the epistle is recognized, as perhaps it should be,[136] as a Christian hymn which the author has adapted much as he did the hymn which serves as the core of the gospel prologue and in which also there is an apparent appeal to eye-witness testimony (Jn. 1, 14). In any case, if we accept the text of the gospel at face value, we appear to be constrained to grant that the evangelist, who is the beloved disciple (mentioned only in the latter part of the gospel: 13, 23; 19, 26; 20, 2), knew Jesus.

The gospel and the first epistle reflect a strong dualism on the basis of which some have maintained that John was directly influenced by the thought of Qumran or, alternatively, that he was a converted Gnostic.[137] This dualism is seen, of course, in John's predilection for the antithesis: light versus darkness (Jn. 1, 5; 3, 19–21; 5, 38; 8, 12; 9, 4–5; 11, 9; 12, 35–36. 46; 1 Jn. 1, 5–7; 2, 8–11), an opposition found in both the writings of the Qumran sect and in later Gnostic works. The Qumranic dualism, however, is ethical, while that of the Gnostics is physical, and John clearly intends an opposition between malice and love (cf. 1 Jn. 2, 9–11) rather than a contrast between a created world which is inherently evil and uncreated divine spirit which is pure. This brings his thought into line with that of Qumran and distinguishes it from Gnosis. John even uses unusual phrases such as "sons of light" (Jn. 12, 36), "spirit of truth," and "spirit of error" (1 Jn. 4, 6) which we also find in the sectarian documents from the Dead Sea. But it would be a mistake to build hypotheses about John's early connections with this sect or with John the Baptist—who may have had some relationship to it—upon these similarities.[138] The kind of ethical dualism to which the evangelist gives expression was common property among the Jews of that period,[139] and John's fondness for the antitheses "light and darkness," "sight and blindness," can be attributed to the use Jesus himself made of them (cf. Mt. 6, 22–23, which is a striking parallel to Jn. 9; Mt. 15, 14; 23, 16–26).

That John was acquainted with distinctively Gnostic speculation, however, seems beyond dispute. R. McL. Wilson finds "some of the clearest traces in the New Testament of an incipient Gnosticism" in the First Epistle of John.[140] The insistence on the reality of Christ's human nature (1 Jn. 4, 2; 2 Jn. 7) and on the identity of the Jesus who was baptized with the Jesus who was crucified (1 Jn. 5, 6 [141]), the allusions to an "anointing" received by the Christian which precludes the need for any "deceptive" teaching from other quarters (1 Jn. 2, 26–27 [142]), and references to those who say they "know" God but disregard moral standards (1 Jn. 2, 4) or who view themselves as an elite which can dispense with the word of Christ (2 Jn. 9) are very solid indications of John's familiarity with the kind of Gnosis associated with Cerinthus.[143] Indeed, there were two drastically different traditions in antiquity about Cerinthus and his relationship to the author of the fourth gospel, but at least they were agreed on the fact of association. What we may conclude from this is that John was exposed to Gnosticism of a Cerinthian variety in one of the Roman empire's great centers of ideological cross-fertilization.

101

The two short epistles of John (2 Jn. and 3 Jn.) give us more information. Both of them indicate that "the presbyter," as he calls himself, was a man of considerable influence. In one letter (2 Jn.) he writes to a Christian community [144] which he obviously regards as prepared to heed his advice, and in the other (3 Jn.) he manifests confidence in the power of his personal presence to neutralize a formidable body of opposition. By the same token, this third epistle precludes identification of the author with the son of Zebedee. It is really inconceivable that *any* opposition to one of the Twelve could exist in a Christian community near the close of the first century. The Apocalypse which, if it does not ante-date, can surely not be later than the Johannine letter, reveals the awesome stature the Twelve had achieved in Christian eyes before the end of the first century: the wall of the new Jerusalem "coming down out of heaven from God" has twelve foundations bearing the "names of the twelve apostles of the Lamb" (Rev. 21, 2. 14). A half century earlier Paul could withstand Cephas (Peter) to his face (Gal. 2, 11), but who was Diotrephes to withstand a "Son of Thunder"? No, the presbyter, for all his authority, could be subjected to abuse (3 Jn. 9), and any effort to identify presbyter and apostle founders on this rock of hard fact.[145]

From the appendix we learn that the evangelist was not expected to die before the Parousia (Jn. 21, 23). Based on a misunderstanding of certain engimatic words of Jesus to Peter (21, 20–22), this belief was fostered, it would seem, by the longevity of the beloved disciple. When, finally, he died, his disciples found it necessary to correct the erroneous report.

To sum up: if the gospel and three epistles are taken as coming from one man, they indicate that the evangelist, whose name of John appears to have been associated with the gospel from at least the first half of the second century, had formerly been a priest or Levite with Sadduceean leanings and connections. He was a Palestinian Jew probably from Jerusalem or some nearby town. He was known to Jesus and witnessed the crucifixion. He had also, apparently, been present at the Last Supper and at the discovery of the empty tomb, but he was not one of the Twelve. He spent enough time, subsequently, in one of the metropolitan centers of the Roman Empire to familiarize himself with an early form of Gnosticism. Ultimately, he became an important figure in an area where he was known as the "presbyter." He died at an advanced age. These conclusions cannot be termed certain, but in varying degrees they all are probable and must be taken into account when dealing with the external testimonies regarding the authorship of the gospel.

The Evangelist: What the Ancient Traditions Tell Us

The list of the testimonies regarding the authorship of the fourth gospel could be a very long one. But those later than the first half of the third century are merely reiterations of the earlier references.

As stated previously, Irenaeus is the first to write about John the evangelist. He tells us several things. (1) The fourth gospel was written by "John the disciple of the Lord, he who had also leaned upon his breast" in Ephesus. (2) The gospel was written to counteract the heresies of Cerinthus and the Nicolaitans. (3) The beloved disciple was personally remembered by Polycarp of Smyrna, whom Irenaeus in turn had known in his youth. (4) From Polycarp Irenaeus received the story of John's hasty exit from the baths in Ephesus upon learning of the presence there of Cerinthus. (5) John lived until the time of Trajan.[146] Two things must be noted. Irenaeus does not say that he received the information about the authorship of the gospel from anyone, and it may well be that he arrived at this conclusion from the fact that the gospel was attributed to John (as we already observed with respect to Theophilus) and that the evangelist was one who, as the gospel itself states, had leaned upon the breast of Jesus (Jn. 21, 20). Nowhere in his writings does Irenaeus call John the son of Zebedee, and although he once or twice *implies* that he was an apostle, that term was broad enough to cover any early Christian missionary, such as Barnabas, to whom it was freely given.[147] Nevertheless, it is most likely that Irenaeus did take for granted the identification of the beloved disciple with the son of Zebedee. The story of John and Cerinthus requires further and separate treatment.

Within something like a decade another important testimony appeared: that of Polycrates, bishop of Ephesus. Writing to Pope Victor with the purpose of substantiating the prestige of the Church in Asia, he points to those illustrious men buried in his own city: Philip the apostle and his daughters,[148] and John, "who had leaned upon the breast of the Lord, who had been a priest wearing the *petalon,* both a martyr and a teacher." [149] He does not say that this John wrote the gospel, but it is obvious both from his use of the phrase—used also by Irenaeus—that John had "leaned upon the breast" of the Lord, and from the epithet "teacher" that this was to be taken for granted. The two other interesting items in this account, the references to John as a "priest" and "martyr" will be discussed below. It is not without some significance that Polycrates refers to John *after* he has mentioned Philip, and that although he has, perhaps incorrectly, designated

Philip as an apostle, he does not claim this distinction for John. It may have seemed superfluous to him, but this would be much clearer if the order of reference to the "great lights" who were buried there was reversed. Something similar occurs in the so-called *Muratorian Canon,* an early Roman list of canonical books compiled possibly by Hippolytus.[150] In this too the John who writes the gospel is called a "disciple," although in the same context "Andrew, one of the apostles," is inspired to approve John's undertaking.

As we have seen, Clement of Alexandria knows of John as the author of the fourth gospel, and from the very interesting story about John which he includes in his little work *What Rich Man May Be Saved?,* it is clear that for him John was one of the apostles.[151] The story of John and the young bandit is so redolent of the gospel and the three epistles—without being in the least contrived—as virtually to guarantee its provenance from a source close to the evangelist. There is the same impression of a man wielding extensive influence over a number of Christian communities which he visits at regular intervals (cp. 2 Jn. 12; 3 Jn. 10. 14), the same admiration for vigorous young men (cp. 1 Jn. 2, 14), and a remarkable parallel to the raising of Lazarus (Jn. 11) in the description of John's rehabilitation of the wayward youth. The one jarring note in the story is the date given for the events recounted: some time after A.D. 96. To this we must return.

The final testimony to be considered is that of Tertullian. Like Clement he identifies the evangelist with the apostle,[152] but he has a further story about John which is

106

peculiar to him. John, he tells us, was subjected to a designedly lethal torture in Rome from which he escaped uninjured.[153] This Roman tradition is singular in that it locates John, for a time at least, in the imperial capital. As with all of the other testimonies, Tertullian's contains an element—specifically the mention of Roman residence—which points to a person other than the son of Zebedee.

The tradition received by Irenaeus, includes the story of John and Cerinthus in the baths at Ephesus, but according to Hippolytus, Cerinthus was an Egyptian,[154] and the setting for that incident, if it actually occurred, is more likely to have been in Alexandria than Ephesus.[155] Polycrates speaks of John as one who had been a priest wearing the *petalon*. P. Nautin, in his scholarly analysis of this document,[156] shows that this curious allusion cannot be interpreted in some metaphorical way, as though it meant that John was a sort of metropolitan archbishop over the churches of Asia.[157] Polycrates meant what he said, just as he meant that John was a martyr [158]—not just a "witness"—and this means that the John buried in Ephesus had been, or at least was believed to have been, a Jewish priest. This agrees entirely, of course, with the first conclusion drawn from the contents of the gospel itself. It does not at all fit the picture of the son of Zebedee given in the New Testament (cf. esp. Acts 4, 13). Finally, there is the difficulty created by Clement of Alexandria's belief that John the apostle is the hero of his otherwise quite credible story. The son of Zebedee in A.D. 96 would have been at least that many years old, yet he is pictured there as ready, at a moment's notice, to ride off on horseback into the hills.[159]

This might be conceivable in the case of a robust septuagenarian, but there are limits to the capacities of even the hardiest nonagenarian!

These traditions agree in attributing the fourth gospel to John, the disciple who leaned upon the Lord's breast and who died in Ephesus, but taken together they also point to someone who had lived in Egypt and in Rome, who was of priestly origin, and who was younger than any one of the Twelve could have been.

The Evangelist: A Plausible Harmonization

We know of another John from the New Testament who deserves very serious consideration as the individual to whom the internal and external evidence given above points; this is John Mark.[160] A resident of Jerusalem with means (Acts 12, 12–13) and a relative of Barnabas (Col. 4, 10) who was a Levite (Acts 4, 36), he may well have been of priestly origin. That he was such is expressly stated in several ancient documents, one of which employs the same phraseology used by Polycrates regarding the beloved disciple: "among the Jewish people he wore the *petalon* of the priestly mitre." [161] His mother Mary was evidently a leading convert, and inasmuch as their home was used as a meeting place for the nascent Christian community (Acts 12, 12), it had very likely been the setting for the Last Supper, in which case John Mark becomes the householder of Mk. 14, 14 and, as host, the person privileged to recline next to Jesus at the meal (Jn. 13, 23). It is significant that Peter goes directly to John Mark's house after escaping from prison rather than to the home of James (who subsequently assumes the leadership of the church in Jerusalem: Acts 12, 17; 15, 13–21; 21, 18; Gal. 2, 12) insofar as this implies a close association between Peter and John Mark (cp. Jn 13, 23–24; 18, 15–16; 20, 2–8; 21, 7. 20–22). As a younger man than either of them, John Mark accompanies Paul and Barnabas on their first missionary journey in the capacity of assistant (Acts 13, 5). John (Luke uses only his Jewish name here) leaves Paul and Barnabas at Perge in Pamphylia, however, and returns to Jerusalem (Acts 13, 13), an action which won for him Paul's disdain (Acts 15, 37–38) and led, ultimately, to a parting of the ways between Paul and Barnabas (Acts 15, 39). John Mark now becomes the companion of Barnabas and the two of them set sail for Cyprus (Acts 15, 39) in or near A.D. 50. Barnabas is mentioned by Paul in his first letter to the Corinthians (1 Cor. 9, 6), which may be dated to 57 A.D., but this is the last reference to him in the New Testament. The *Clementine Homilies* [162] give an account of missionary activity by Barnabas in Alexandria, while the apocryphal *Acts of Barnabas* [163]—a work considered far more reliable than most of its kind—states that John Mark sailed for Alexandria after the brutal lynching of Barnabas in Cyprus. John Mark does reappear in the New Testament. Writing probably from Rome in 61 A.D., Paul mentions him in two of his letters (Col. 4, 10; Philem. 24). It is interesting to note that the two men had reconciled their differences, but the consequences of the original rift still lingered, as we realize from the need Paul felt to insist that John Mark be received by the Colossians, who had been given "special instructions" about him (Col. 4, 10). We cannot but be reminded here of the situation which called forth the third Johannine epistle: the refusal of Diotrephes to receive the presbyter.

The final notice of John Mark in the New Testament comes again from Paul.[164] Writing to Timothy, the apostle urges him to come to Rome before winter and to bring Mark with him, "for he is most useful in serving my needs" (2 Tim. 4, 11. 21). Time had vindicated John Mark, though not necessarily in the eyes of lesser men than Paul. In any case, it is at Ephesus where he is last to be found.

There is no need to labor the apposite way in which the available information about John Mark dovetails with the details we have accepted for an authentic portrait of the author of the fourth gospel and three Johannine epistles. What requires some explanation is the absence of any ancient attestation to this identification. Perhaps this can best be handled by first asking a number of other questions. (1) How is it that the learned Dionysius of Alexandria, for all his knowledge of the scriptures, professes an ignorance of John Mark beyond what is stated in Acts 12–13? [165] (2) Why does St. John Chrysostom hesitate to identify John Mark and end by suggesting that he is, in fact, John the apostle? [166] (3) What accounts for the fact that by the ninth century in such widely separated centers as Constantinople and Saragossa, and in quite different ways, the identity of John Mark has been obliterated and the son of Zebedee put in his place? [167] (4) What is to be made of the newly discovered letter of Clement of Alexandria in which reference is made to a gospel by Mark which includes a parallel account of John's narration of the raising of Lazarus? [168] The only answer which can satisfy all these questions is that the memory of John Mark faded, partly because he had been a controversial and probably an unpopular figure in his lifetime, and partly because the two names he bore, John and Mark, led to a widespread confusion with the son of Zebedee on one hand, and with the author of the *second* gospel on the other.[169] If John Mark *is* the fourth evangelist, that can also be the only explanation for the absence of ancient testimonies to that effect.[170] However, perhaps we *do* have a trace of a soon forgotten tradition that John Mark wrote the fourth gospel. Apart from the apocryphal *Acts of Barnabas* mentioned above, the fullest account of John Mark to be found outside the New Testament is in the sixth-century *Praise of the Apostle Barnabas* by Alexander the Monk.[171] Like the apocryphal *Acts,* this work preserves much older Cypriot traditions.[172] In it the house of John Mark becomes the background of the Lord's Jerusalem ministry as we follow it in the fourth gospel. In other words, the fourth gospel unfolds as only John Mark could have made it do so. This is the implication behind Alexander's statements. A similar inference might also be drawn from the less impressive Arabic history of the patriarchs of Alexandria.

John Mark, Mark, John the Prophet, John the Presbyter

To identify John Mark with the beloved disciple entails some discussion of Mark the evangelist. Generally speaking, modern commentators do not distinguish Mark from John Mark, though there are notable exceptions.[174] But this identification does not rest on very sure foundations. The earliest witness to it is the clumsy Monarchian prologue to the second gospel.[175] Papias, on the other hand, testified that Mark, Peter's faithful disciple (cf. 1 Pet. 5, 13), had never heard Jesus, and the Muratorian canon clearly implies that he had never even seen the Lord.[176] It is hard to reconcile these statements with what can be surmised about John Mark. Moreover, it is evident from St. Jerome's cautious acceptance of the identification [177] that it was certainly not taken for granted in the fifth century. The liturgical practice of the Greek Church has always distinguished Mark from John Mark.[178] On the other hand, it has been suggested [179] that both the second and the fourth gospel come from the same individual (at widely separated periods of his life), and it may be that such a view will find support in the still unpublished letter of Clement of Alexandria to Theodore.

Something must also be said about the John who wrote the Apocalypse. He numbers himself among the "prophets" of the early Church (Rev. 22, 8–9), and just as surely excludes himself from the august circle of the Twelve (Rev. 21, 14). Justin Martyr, at an early date, does call him an apostle of Jesus Christ, [180] but this term was never coextensive with that of the "Twelve." Justin apparently locates this John at Ephesus,[181] which would suggest that he may have been the beloved disciple. That conclusion was indeed drawn, but not without first having been vigorously opposed; the arguments of Dionysius of Alexandria retain their persuasiveness to the present day.[182] Dionysius also gives it as his understanding that there were two Johns buried in Ephesus, and the *Apostolic Constitutions* indirectly echo this.[183] Papias, in a passage which has been trotted out times beyond number in support of one or another contradictory position, speaks of his conscientious effort to collect the oral traditions of "the elders," those men who had listened to the apostles. Among the elders are two he specifically names: Aristion and John.[184] The latter is given as the source of an apocalyptic saying (supposedly dominical in origin) about the fruitfulness of the messianic kingdom.[185] If it is representative of his theological orientation, he could well be the author of the apocalypse. At the same time, some connection between "the prophet" and the evangelist John is suggested by the presence of certain key terms in both the gospel and the

114

Apocalypse, and by the liturgical elements which are so marked a feature of both.[186] Stylistically and theologically the works could not be more diverse.

We may suppose that the prophet, arriving at Ephesus from Patmos, attached himself to the aged evangelist whose influence is faintly discernible in the Book of Revelations. With his encouragement he forwards his searing indictment of the Roman empire to the great churches of Asia Minor (Rev. 2–3).

These are nothing more than educated guesses, but the complicated questions at issue scarcely permit anything more. Our information about the history of the Church in its first century and of the personalities who shaped it remains exasperatingly disparate and inadequate.

EXCURSUS

Gnostic, Indian, and Early Christian Religious Thought in Alexandria

We have seen that the author of 1 John, whom we take to be John the beloved disciple and evangelist, alludes to Gnostic views and terms, and we have accordingly concluded that he was an informed and traveled citizen of the Hellenistic world in which he lived. It has also been suggested that John adapted certain Mahayana Buddhist ways of expression to his own theology. What verifiable circumstances lend credibility to these conjectures?

The origins of Gnosticism are currently the subject of intense debate and research. The difficulty is not in recognizing the sources of the manifold constitutive elements, but in fixing the time and place of their synthesis. The problem is aggravated by the fact that synthesis did not occur in one specific way or at one specific time and place. Gnosticism grew and presented, if not a different

116

face, a different complexion in different areas and at different intervals.[187] Nevertheless, the more important early forms of Gnosticism took shape in the two great imperial centers of intellectual ferment: Alexandria and Rome.[188] Egypt seems to have offered particularly fertile soil for Gnosticism,[189] as the impressive list of Egyptian Gnostic teachers reveals: Cerinthus, Basilides, Carpocrates, Isidore, Valentinus. This can hardly be surprising. Apart from its reputation as a center of learning, Alexandria was ideally situated geographically to receive the wares—material and spiritual—of East and West, and Gnosticism was a syncretistic phenomenon.[190]

It is acknowledged with increasing frequency today that an interaction between Gnostic and Indian religious thought must be posited.[191] Common to both, of course, is the conviction that a correct insight into the nature of the world liberates man from it and effects some kind of reunion with the Transcendent, which is, ultimately, none other than the true self. But beyond this fundamental premise shared alike by Gnostics, Hindus, and Buddhists, Edward Conze has described eight basic similarities between Gnosticism and Mahayana Buddhism in particular, similarities which, he insists, pertain to the essential structure of the respective systems and not to anything peripheral.[192] What he and others find impossible to answer satisfactorily at present is the question of the direction taken by such influence.[193] But that Egypt provided the principal point of contact cannot be doubted. A colony of Indians existed at Memphis as early as 200 B.C.,[194] by which time commerce between Egypt and India was es-

117

tablished on a regular basis.[195] At the end of the first century A.D., Dio Chrysostom, addressing the Alexandrians, made reference to the "Indians who view the spectacles with you and are in your midst on all occasions." [196] Neither can it be doubted that specifically Indian doctrines reached Alexandria. Filliozat points out that Hippolytus' exposition of brahmanic speculation discloses an informed knowledge of specific texts rather than a superficial acquaintance with mere generalities.[197] Hippolytus, it must be noted, had probably come to Rome from Alexandria.[198]

As the relevant passage in Hippolytus' *Philosophoumena* shows, the educated Christian was as interested in Indian philosophy as were his pagan counterparts, Gnostic or otherwise. In fact, there is much to indicate that during the first few centuries of the Christian era, Christian and Buddhist, where exposed to one another, exerted some measure of reciprocal influence. (1) The striking similarity between some details in the Mahayanist *Prajnaparamita* and those found in the Apocalypse (roughly contemporary documents). Conze, who has called attention to these, believes they point to a Mediterranean-based Christian influence on Mahayanist literature.[199] (2) The tradition recorded by Eusebius and repeated by Jerome [200] that Pantaenus, the teacher of Clement of Alexandria and the latter's predecessor as director of the Christian Academy in Alexandria,[201] traveled as far as India, where he was asked to explain his faith to the Brahmins.[202] (3) Clement of Alexandria's references to the Buddha which, though *obiter dicta,* are, as de Lubac notes, "as much, if not more than anything to be found elsewhere." [203] (4) Hippolytus' familiarity with Indian speculation referred to above. (5) The parallels between Mahayanist teaching and certain passages in the writings of Origen.[204] In the judgment of de Lubac these are not illusory and may be the result of an actual exchange of ideas.[205] (6) This judgment is reenforced by Benz's contention that Ammonius Sacca, the Alexandrian philosopher who taught Longinus, Origen, and Plotinus, was another Buddhist monk of the tribe of the Sakya from which Gotama himself had arisen.[206] (7) Such Buddhist influence on Origen is accepted by Cornelis with respect to other aspects of Origen's thought,[207] and Cornelis also finds Gregory of Nyssa's view of corporeality "strangely reminiscent" of the Buddhist *samsara*.[208] Gregory was, of course, an intellectual heir of Origen.

This interesting list of considerations furnishes us with evidence of continuous contact between Indian and Christian thinkers from at least the end of the first to the end of the third century. It also justifies the hypothesis that in a city like Alexandria the fourth evangelist was as likely to have heard Buddhist teaching as Gnostic. It is *more* than likely that the two went hand in hand and appealed to the same circles, so that to learn of one was to learn of the other.

NOTES

1. R. E. Brown's commentary, *The Gospel According to St. John* (*Anchor Bible* series, no. 29 [New York, 1966]), of which only the first part (I-XII) has been published to date, leaves nothing to be desired. He has read everything relevant and given all views and interpretations a fair hearing. It is the most important commentary on John by a Catholic scholar since Lagrange first published his volume in 1925 and, when completed, will represent a monumental study of the gospel.

2. R. E. Schnackenburg, another Roman Catholic scholar, published the first volume of his commentary: *Das Johannesevangelium 1 Teil, Herders Theologischer Kommentar zum Neuen Testament IV* (Freiburg, 1965). The English translation, by Kevin Smyth, appeared in 1968: *The Gospel According to St. John, Vol. 1* (London and New York). This volume covers introductory questions and the first four chapters of the gospel (the English edition runs to 638 pages). It is an important work and often profound, but less comprehensive and slightly less open to opposing interpretations than is Brown's.

3. Another new full-scale commentary by the late Dean J. N. Sanders and B. A. Mastin has just appeared (*A Commentary on the Gospel According to St. John, Black's New Testament Commentaries* [London, 1968]), as has a provocative study by J. L. Martyn (*History and Theology in the Fourth Gospel* [New York, 1968]). Short studies by A. M. Hunter (*According to John* [London, 1968]), N. Micklem (*Behold the Man* [London, 1969]), and W. H. Cadman (*The Open Heaven* [New York, 1969]), are equally recent.

4. Cf. M. F. Wiles, *The Spiritual Gospel: The Interpretation of the Fourth Gospel in the Early Church* (Cambridge, 1960).

5. By "John" I mean the evangelist without at this point assuming anything about his identity; for this reason also I omit the title "saint." Oc-

120

casionally, as here, "John" will stand for the gospel rather than for the individual. In Part Three I will attempt to identify the evangelist but without any illusions as to the extent to which this attempt will satisfy my readers.

6. A. M. Hunter (*op. cit.*) deals clearly and succinctly with the present state of Johannine studies, though he tends to emphasize the Judaic character of John at the expense of the Hellenistic. His brief chapter (pp. 49–55) on topography in John is somewhat simplistic but gives a good idea of the importance of topography in the gospel in terms of evaluating the evangelist's factual knowledge.

7. Such as that of the healing of the paralytic in chapter five, as will be made clear in Part Two. H. van der Loos, who denies the use of symbolism by the fourth evangelist (*The Miracles of Jesus,* [Leiden, 1965], pp. 588–589, 609–618), empties the gospel of any serious theology.

8. H. van den Bussche (*Jean,* [Bruges, 1967]) is not disposed to find symbolism in John (cf. pp. 42, 44), but neither does he find any evidence of literary craftsmanship in the gospel: *"Nulle trace de recherche artistique, aucun effort pour enjoliver l'expression"* (p. 7), a view totally at variance with the one to be presented here and also, it would seem, with his own conception of the evangelist's style as *"hiératique"* (p. 8).

9. Cf. Wiles, *op. cit.,* pp. 22–40. Theodore's literalism, Wiles shows, can betray him "into comments which show a complete misunderstanding of the text."

10. Cf. J. R. Diaz, "Palestinian Targum and the New Testament," *NovT,* 6 (1963), 76f.

11. This is an extreme position but I do not think it is unjustified. If some details are *unmistakably* included because they possess more than a literal, factual value (as even someone like van den Bussche will admit [*op. cit.,* p. 44]), then all details *probably* have this twofold value. Obviously, any detail in any piece of literature *may* have more than one meaning, but possibility becomes probability when we see that an author is disposed, inclined, to use a device of this sort. Probability, it seems to me, yields to moral certainty when *every* detail included in a work on the author's initiative (therefore not part of a received tradition) has in context a *truly appropriate* symbolic significance; and in the case of the fourth gospel we come so close to finding this true that the one or two exceptions (for example, Jn. 11, 54) should be treated as *apparent* exceptions whose symbolism is merely lost to *us*.

12. *Op. cit.,* p. 1.

13. *The Johannine Epistles* (London, 1946). He published his arguments previously in article form ("The First Epistle of John and the Fourth Gospel," *BJRylL,* 21 [1937], 129–156). It is not to be thought that Dodd was the first to question unity of authorship. Actually, an official document of the Church (the *Decretum Gelasianum* of the fifth century) distinguished between John the presbyter, the author of 2 and 3 John, and the apostle John, the author of the gospel and the first

epistle (cf. *EB,* 19), and so did St. Jerome (*De viris illustribus,* 18). Nineteenth-century discussion of the question is outlined by A. E. Brooke in his commentary, *The Johannine Epistles* (ICC [Edinburgh, 1912] i-xxvii), but, as can be seen from his conclusions, the arguments against unity of authorship were generally discounted. In raising the question anew, Dodd did not introduce any significant new ones.

14. "The Common Authorship of the Johannine Gospel and Epistles," *JTS,* 48 (1947), 12–25. See also T. W. Manson, "The Fourth Gospel," in *Studies in the Gospels and Epistles* (Philadelphia, 1962), pp. 105–122.

15. In any consideration of Dodd's position one must be more impressed by the list of quite ordinary words missing in the epistle but frequent in the gospel than by the list of such favorite gospel terms as *"doxa"* ("glory") or *"hypsouthai"* ("lift up") which are almost exclusively placed on the lips of Jesus in the gospel. But the presence or absence of ordinary words in the epistle and gospel seems also to be due to the difference of literary genre. There is no narrative in the epistle; it is all discourse. The word *"oun"* ("therefore") does not appear once in the epistle, although it occurs 190 times in the gospel. But an analysis of chapters 13–20 of the gospel (a section containing both narrative and discourse) shows that of the 73 times *"oun"* is used, only *once* (16, 22) does it fall in the context of discourse. That it should not occur at all in the epistle, which is less than half the length of Jn. 13–20, is hardly surprising.

16. There were three annual pilgrimage festivals in the Israelite calendar: Tabernacles, Passover, and Pentecost (Weeks). A pious Jew was expected to "go up" to Jerusalem for these feasts if he could do so. John does not fail to mention Passover and Tabernacles when they enter into his narrative (Jn. 2, 13; 6, 4; 7, 2; 11, 55 etc.) even when Jesus does *not* go up to Jerusalem (Jn. 6). But here we are told that Jesus "went up" to Jerusalem for an unnamed feast. Pentecost is surely intended. John's failure to name it may be seen as an accurate reflection of the relative neglect of this festival by the Jews of his time. Cf. R. de Vaux, *Les Institutions de l'Ancien Testament II* (Paris, 1960) pp. 396–397. The feast *"n'eut jamais qu'une importance secondaire."*

17. Cf. M. E. Boismard, *Du Baptême à Cana* (Paris, 1956). The case for seven days hinges on acceptance of the variant reading *"mane"* ("in the early morning") at 1, 41. Boismard has since reversed his judgment ("Les traditions johanniques concernant le Baptiste," *RB,* 70 [1963], 5–42), but not every one will want to follow suit.

18. Cf. T. Barrosse, "The Seven Days of the New Creation in St. John's Gospel," *CBQ,* 21 (1959), 507–516.

19. A feast of Dionysus was celebrated on January 6th, and miraculous effusions of wine were believed to take place on that day: cf. O. Cullmann, "The Origin of Christmas," in *The Early Church* (London, 1956), pp. 24–25; C. K. Barrett, *The Gospel According to St. John* (London, 1954), p. 158. This was apparently transformed into the Christian feast

122

of the Epiphany, but at what date it is hard to say. So far as evidence exists the earliest known observance of it was among Egyptian Gnostic Christians (cf. Clement of Alexandria, *Stromata,* 1, 21). We would have to suppose—if John 1, 19—2, 1 is meant to point to January 6th—that the evangelist intended to portray Jesus at 2, 7–11 as the *true* Dionysus. Barrett (*ibid.*) does not reject the possibility, and J. Estlin Carpenter (*The Johannine Writings* [London, 1927], p. 380) favors it, but Schnackenburg (*The Gospel According to St. John,* p. 340) rules it out of consideration.

20. Cf. M. E. Boismard, "Le chapitre xxi de Saint Jean," *RB,* 54 (1947), 473–501.

21. This theme is dealt with at length by J. Daniélou, *Bible et Liturgie* (Paris, 1951), pp. 355–387 (ET *The Bible and the Liturgy* [Notre Dame, 1956], pp. 262–286). Cf. also H. Rahner, *Greek Myths and Christian Mystery* (New York, 1963), pp. 74–78. References to the "eighth day" appear in the *Epistle of Barnabas* (xv, 8–9) and in Justin Martyr's *Dialogue with Trypho* (xxiv, 1), both of which date to about 130 A.D. (the Dialogue took place at that time, though it was written down somewhat later).

22. The three great pilgrimage festivals were originally argicultural feasts, but each one in turn was "historicized," that is, adapted so as to commemorate the principal events of the Exodus: Passover, the departure from Egypt; Tabernacles, God's providential care of the Israelites in the wilderness; and Pentecost, the giving of the Law on Sinai. Passover and Tabernacles were "historicized" during the biblical period, but the earliest clear signs of the process at work in the case of Pentecost are to be found in the intertestamental *Book of Jubilees* and in the sectarian writings of Qumran. Nevertheless, it had acquired its association with the giving of the Law by the time this gospel was written. Cf. T. Maertens, *C'est fête en l'honneur de Yahvé* (Bruges, 1961), pp. 113–127.

23. An excellent summary of the state of the question and some very sound principles of interpretation are given by R. E. Brown, "The Johannine Sacramentary Reconsidered," in his *New Testament Essays* (London, 1967), pp. 51–76.

24. *New Testament Theology* (London, 1963), p. 41 and Appendix II, pp. 334–338.

25. Cf. n. 20 above.

26. Cf. L. Vaganay, "La Finale du Quatrième Évangile," *RB,* 45 (1936), 512–528. In this valuable study Vaganay arrives at the conclusion that 20, 30–31 stood originally at the end of chapter 21 on the basis of patristic texts.

27. The copyist of the codex *Sinaiticus* omitted it, though a later hand "corrected" this omission.

28. Cf. Vaganay, *op. cit.,* 524.

29. In talking of the fourth gospel Origen remarks that John "left

only one gospel, to be sure, though he admits that he could have written so many books that the world itself could not contain them" (Eusebius, *Historia Ecclesiastica,* 6, 25). Origen here has simply cited Jn. 21, 25 in the third person.

30. *Op. cit.,* p. 379.

31. *The Gospel According to St. John,* pp. 414, 427–430, 469, 480.

32. In 1958 Professor Morton Smith of Columbia University discovered a copy of a hitherto unknown letter attributed to Clement of Alexandria in which reference is made to a supplementary gospel of Mark's (written in Alexandria after the death of Peter) containing an episode parallel to Jn. 11. A preliminary report of this discovery was made to the 96th Meeting of the Society of Biblical Literature and Exegesis in New York City on December 29th, 1960, and reported in *The New York Times* the next day. Professor Smith has prepared a monograph soon to be released on this enormously important discovery. It will be of great interest to New Testament scholars to learn, among other things, where this miracle is situated, chronologically, in the "deutero-Markan" gospel.

33. Cf. A. Feuillet, "Les thèmes bibliques majeurs du discours sur le pain de vie (Jn. 6)," *NRT,* 82 (1960), 803–822, 918–939, 1040–1062; M. E. Boismard, "Le Lavement des pieds," *RB,* 71 (1964), 5–24.

34. So R. E. Brown (*The Gospel According to St. John,* p. 376). J. L. Martyn (*op. cit.,* p. 3) begins his study of the gospel with chapter 9 because he finds its construction "particularly inviting" to those who want to distinguish between what John has received and what is his own work. C. K. Barrett considers Jn. 9 the best expression of the evangelist's "conception of the work of Christ" (*op. cit.,* p. 293). More generally, E. Burrows noted that John is "an artist of 'scenes,' the creator of extraordinary mystic effects" (*The Gospel of the Infancy and Other Biblical Essays* [London, 1940], p. 52 n. 2).

35. M.-J. Lagrange, *Évangile selon Saint Jean* (Paris, 1948), p. 399. Of the parable of the vine and the branches he says: *"on le placerait très naturellement après le choix des disciples—apôtres et avant leur première mission."* The motif would harmonize well with the miracle of the water changed into wine.

36. "La signification théologique du second miracle de Cana (Jn. 4, 46–54," *RechSR,* 48 (1960), 62–75.

37. Cf. Barrett, *op. cit.,* p. 232–233.

38. Like the "foot washing" episode at Jn. 13, 4–15, the anointing offers an occasion for sacramental teaching which B. Vawter believes is implicit in it ("The Johannine Sacramentary," *TS,* 17 (1956), 151–166).

39. As, from a deeply Christian point of view, has also Teilhard de Chardin in his writings, especially in *The Divine Milieu* (New York, 1960).

40. The Sadducees did not believe in the doctrine of bodily resurrection, which they regarded as a Pharisaic innovation (cf. Mk. 12, 18–27

and synoptic parallels). Not all Jewish priests were Sadducees, of course, but rather only those who belonged to what we would call "the upper crust," and not even all of these (Flavius Josephus, the historian, is an outstanding example of a priest from the very highest stratum of Judaic society who embraced Pharisaic beliefs).

41. D. de Bruyne ("Les Plus Anciens Prologues Latins des Evangiles," *RevBen,* 40 [1928], 207) assigned an early date (the second half of the second century), but more recently R. G. Heard ("The Old Gospel Prologues," *JTS,* 6 [N.S. 1955], 14–15) argues for a date in the fifth "or even the sixth century."

42. The prologue claims to derive its information from Papias, which is scarcely credible inasmuch as Eusebius, who had the writings of Papias before him, knew of no such attestation by Papias regarding the authorship of the fourth gospel. The dates of Papias are approximately 70–140 A.D.

43. Wiles (*op. cit.,* p. 7) thinks the prologue implies that the gospel "had something of the character of a last Will and Testament of the aged disciple."

44. As quoted by Eusebius (*Hist. Eccl.,* VI, 14).

45. Irenaeus affirms that the gospel was written to confound the heresies of Cerinthus and the Nicolaitans (*Adversus Haereses,* III, 11, 7). For various hypotheses cf. H. L. Jackson, *The Problem of the Fourth Gospel* (Cambridge, 1918), pp. 127–128.

46. Contrast J. A. T. Robinson, "The Destination and the Purpose of St. John's Gospel," *NTS,* 6 (1959–60), 117–131, with C. H. Dodd, *The Interpretation of the Fourth Gospel* (Cambridge, 1960), pp. 8f.; and R. H. Lightfoot, *St. John's Gospel* (Oxford, 1956), pp. 50ff.

47. *Op. cit.,* p. 115. Jackson (*op. cit.,* pp. 128–129) in a similar vein suggests that the evangelist quite possibly "never contemplated any immediate publication and circulation of his work," though his disciples would naturally convey the substance of it to "an ever widening circle of receptive minds."

48. Barrett's view of chapters 15–17 as seen above (cf. n. 30). S. Temple's view of 6, 48–59 ("A Key to the Composition of the Fourth Gospel," *JBL,* 80 [1961], 220–232); Schnackenburg's view of 3, 16–21. 31–36 ("Die 'situationsgelösten' Redestücke in Jo 3," *ZNW,* 49 [1958], 88–89).

49. If read with due caution (in all that pertains to her underlying— and presently unverifiable—hypothesis of a triennial lectionary cycle), A. Guilding's *The Fourth Gospel and Jewish Worship* (Oxford, 1960) sheds much light on this aspect of the gospel's composition.

50. With regard to John's use of time see J. E. Bruns, "The Use of Time in the Fourth Gospel", *NTS,* 13 (1966–1967), 285–290.

51. E. Hoskyns, *The Fourth Gospel,* (London, 1947), p. 509.

52. Cf. J. E. Bruns, "A Note on Jn. 12, 3," *CBQ,* 28 (1966), 219–222.

53. See in particular F. M. Braun, *Jean le théologien, 2, Les grands*

traditions d'Israel et l'accord des Écritures selon le quatrième Évangile (Paris, 1964).

54. Cf. H. Strack and P. Billerbeck, *Kommentar zum Neuen Testament aus Talmud und Midrasch* (Munich, 1924), II, pp. 302–387. R. E. Brown, "The Qumran Scrolls and the Johannine Gospel and Epistles," *CBQ,* 17 (1955), 403–419. H. M. Teeple, "Qumran and the Origin of the Fourth Gospel," *NovT,* 4 (1960–1961), 6–25.

55. Cf. C. K. Barrett, "The Theological Vocabulary of the Fourth Gospel and of the Gospel of Truth," in *Current Issues in New Testament Interpretation,* O. A. Piper, ed. (New York, 1962), pp. 210–223.

56. Cf. C. R. Bowen, "The Fourth Gospel as Dramatic Material," *JBL,* 49 (1930), 292–305; E. K. Lee, "The Drama of the Fourth Gospel," *ExpTim,* 65 (1953–1954), 173–176; C. M. Connick, "The Dramatic Character of the Fourth Gospel," *JBL,* 67 (1948), 159–169. That John may have made limited use of the dialogues of Plato as models was suggested by B. H. Streeter (*The Four Gospels: A Study in Origins* [London, 1924], pp. 370–371) and has been upheld more recently by H. A. Guy (*The Gospel and Letters of John* [London, 1963], p. 16).

57. Guy (*ibid.,* p. 31) speaks for all: "He was evidently a cultured and well-educated man, acquainted with contemporary religious and philosophical movements among both Jews and Gentiles."

58. Cf. H. I. Bell, *Egypt from Alexander the Great to the Arab Conquest* (Oxford, 1948; reprinted 1966), pp. 81–82, 143 n. 20.

59. P. W. Harsh, *A Handbook of Classical Drama* (Stanford, 1963), p. 16.

60. Cf. Jn. 2, 20; 3, 4; 4, 11. 33; 6, 42; 7, 35; 8, 22. 52–53; 11, 12–13. 24; 13, 36–37; 14, 4–5. 22; 16, 17–18.

61. On lengthy discourse as a feature of the Greek drama cf. R. W. Livingston, *The Pageant of Greece* (Oxford, 1924), pp. 100ff.; and on the place of dialogue in Greek dramatic structure cf. H. C. Baldry, *Greek Literature for the Modern Reader* (Cambridge, 1951), p. 153. It may be, of course, that *we* are employing anachronistic standards for the evaluation of John's work. In terms of his age, the second type of chapter may have represented a finer literary creation than the first type.

62. Cf. n. 34 above.

63. Guy, *op. cit.,* p. 16.

64. P. Guichou (*Évangile de S. Jean* [Paris, 1962], pp. 57f.) suggests that Nicodemus is the scribe who appears at Mk. 12, 28–34, in which case this episode in John properly belongs to the last week of the public ministry, as Tatian anciently believed. Other views regarding the proper positioning of this pericope are offered by S. Mendner ("Nikodemus," *JBL,* 77 [1958], 293–323) and J. Bligh ("Four Studies in St. John: Nicodemus," *HeythJ,* 8 [1967], 40–51).

65. "The 'Divine Hero' Christology in the New Testament," *HarvTR,* 41 (1948), 229–249.

66. On the vitality and significance of the Heraclean saga from the age of Pindar to the end of paganism cf. A. J. Festugière, *Epicure et ses Dieux* (Paris, 1946), pp. viif.

67. J. E. Bruns. "A Note on John 16, 33 and 1 John 2, 13–14," *JBL*, 86 (1967), 451–453.

68. Reference has already been made to the possibility that John wished to represent Jesus as a *true* Dionysus as well (cf. n. 19 above).

69. Cf. J. E. Bruns, "Some Reflections on Qoheleth and John," *CBQ*, 25 (1963), 414–416.

70. Not surprisingly, this is the sober judgment of the most recent commentator on Ecclesiastes after weighing all the already existing views about Qoheleth's background and education; cf. L. Di Fonzo, *Ecclesiaste* (Rome, 1967), pp. 44–63, 70–74, see esp. pp. 71–72.

71. We have seen that the "first" conclusion of the gospel (20, 31) may well have come at the end of chapter 21 as part of the appendix composed by the disciples (cf. n. 26 above), in which case it would be *their* interpretation of the evangelist's purpose; but they were surely not unfaithful to his thoughts, as a comparison of this verse with 1 Jn. 5, 13 proves.

72. The awkwardness and abruptness of Jn. 3, 2–3 is softened considerably if Guichou's suggestion is adopted (cf. n. 64 above).

73. The Greek reads, literally, "do not wonder [or, marvel] that I said to *thee: you* must be born again." The transition from singular to plural number in the pronoun shows that the words in the latter half of the sentence are not addressed to Nicodemus as an individual but to a wider audience, to mankind; hence my translation, "men must be born again."

74. It is important to realize that in these verses Jesus is not simply telling his listeners how the man inspired by the Spirit will appear to them (as observers), but how the experience they must undergo themselves (if they would "see the kingdom of heaven") will remind them of the movement of the wind.

75. Cf. J. E. Bruns, "The Discourse on the Good Shepherd and the Rite of Ordination," *AER*, 149 (1963), 386–391.

76. We find powerful expressions of it in the prophetical books, for example, Is. 58, 1–7; 66, 1–3; Amos 5, 11–25; Jer. 7, 1–14.

77. So, especially, R. Bultmann, *Life and Death* (London, 1965), pp. 75–76 (Kittel Bible Key Words); *Das Evangelium des Johannes* (Göttingen, 1962), pp. 162, 196–197, 262–263.

78. In the apocryphal but generally well-esteemed *Acts of Paul and Thecla* a similar view is attributed to Demas (probably the Demas of 2 Tim. 4, 10) and Hermogenes, who declare that men "rise again" when they come to the knowledge of the true God (xiv). This, of course, sounds very Johannine, but is represented here (in these *Acts*) as a heretical teaching. For quite other reasons Dom John Chapman sought to identify the Demas of Paul's letters (Col. 4, 14; Philem. 24; 2 Tim.

4, 10) with John's friend Demetrius (3 Jn. 12); cf. "Historical Setting of II and III St. John," *JTS,* 5 (1904), 357–368, 517–534.

79. This view is discussed and rejected by W. F. Howard, *Christianity According to St. John* (London, 1943), pp. 57–80, 106–128.

80. It is interesting to contrast 1 Jn. 3, 2 with 1 Jn. 4, 17, since they represent different perspectives and, at first sight, opposing ones. The second text declares that in this world we are like Jesus as he is *now* (that is, glorified). This bold statement has given rise to difficulties and to variant readings (cf. R. Bultmann, *Die drei Johannesbriefe* [Göttingen, 1967], p. 77), especially because of the seemingly contradictory statement at 3, 2. A more thoughtful reading of the latter text, however, seems to yield this meaning: Beloved, we are now children of God (that is, we have entered eternal life and share the life which Jesus had and still has); what we will be like in other respects (physical) at his coming is not yet evident. But this is of no concern, for the important thing is that when Jesus appears again we will be like him in all respects, since we will see him as he is, and this sight is born of connaturality. Whatever the glorified body is like, it is only an efflorescence of eternal life itself, which we already possess. In such a reading this text conforms well to what we recognize as John's realized eschatology. The question of a future physical state is wholly subordinated to the present possession of eternal life.

81. There is good support for the variant reading: "so that we might know *the true thing"* (or, "that which is true"). It is attested by the codex Sinaiticus, the Coptic (Sahidic), and Old Latin (Freisingen fragment) versions. If John wrote this, it would be an indication of his ability to conceive abstractly of the divine. As will be seen, when he *defines* God, he does so in terms of hypostasized activity.

82. *Adumbrationes in Epist. 1 Joannis (MPG,* 9, 738).

83. This is the meaning of Jn. 1, 51, as we shall see. On this verse cf. Schnackenburg, *The Gospel According to St. John, Vol. 1,* pp. 319–233. It may not seem very satisfactory theologically to desribe the incarnate Word as "the focal point of the divine presence in the world," but one must not expect to find in the New Testament a developed metaphysic about the union of natures in Christ. As we will shortly see, the evangelist did wrestle with the mystery of the person of Christ—and successfully—, but not in fourth- or fifth-century terms.

84. Cf. Strack-Billerbeck, *op. cit.,* I, pp. 495f.; II, pp. 193–197.

85. Cf. Guilding, *op. cit.,* pp. 82–83.

86. So, for example, St. Augustine (*Ennaratio in Pss.,* Ps. 70, 20; Ps. 83, 7). Among modern commentators, Guichou (*op. cit.,* p. 86).

87. Cf. J. Jeremias, *Die Wiederentdeckung von Bethesda (Joh 5, 2)* (Göttingen, 1949). (ET. *The Rediscovery of Bethseda* [Louisville, 1966]); N. Van Der Vliet, *S. Marie où elle est née et la piscine probatique* (Jerusalem and Paris, 1938).

88. Cf. T. F. Glasson, *Moses in the Fourth Gospel* (London, 1963), p. 89.

89. Cp. 1 Jn. 1, 8–9; 2, 3–4. 7–8; 2 Jn. 5–6. John shifts easily from singular to plural and back again, but the singular form is the primary one in his thought, as these texts show.

90. *Op. cit.,* p. 271.

91. Bultmann, *Das Evangelium des Johannes,* p. 537; Barrett, *The Gospel According to St. John,* p. 475.

92. "Le Péché, c'est l'iniquité," *NRT,* 78, (1956), 785–797.

93. *The Testament of Jesus* (London, 1968), p. 63. He refers to the "cutting iciness" of the "so-called apostle of love." Käsemann views the commandment to love in both gospel ad epistle as directed towards those within the community alone (cf. pp. 60–61). He sees 1 Jn. 2, 15 as a sharp contrast to Jn. 3, 16; but we may take Clement of Alexandria's comment on 1 Jn. 5, 19 (*op. cit.,* 9, 738) as being closer to the mind of John: "It is not [the world] as creation [which lies in the power of evil], but worldly men, and then insofar as they pursue [their] lusts."

94. Schnackenburg, for example, states that John's Christology merges *"zu einer einheitlichen Konzeption"* (German edition, p. 447; English edition, p. 556: "a consistent composition"). He speaks of the evangelist achieving a final "amalgamation" of the various elements; but these statements seem unfortunate because he speaks earlier, and more realistically, of the "considerable tensions," Christological and eschatological, in the texts of John (p. 71).

95. Käsemann's view, as presented in *Jesu letzter Wille nach Johannes 17* (Tübingen, 1966; English edition referred to in n. 93 above), is that John has reinterpreted the life of Jesus in terms of a God who walks on earth not subjected to earthly conditions. Consequently, John's eschatology is really *protology,* that is, in Christ the end of the world is present and remains present continually! This slight volume, though highly controversial, is one of the most stimulating contributions to Johannine studies in recent years.

96. Cf. A. Feuillet, "Le Fils de l'homme de Daniel et la tradition biblique," RB, 60 (1963), 337–339.

97. Cf. Enoch, 71, 14.

98. Cf. E. Stauffer, *Jesus and His Story* (New York, 1960), pp. 174–195.

99. Cf. G. Quispel, "Het Johannesevangelie en de Gnosis," *NedTTs* 11 (1956–57), 173–203.

100. Stauffer comes close to this position in his *New Testament Theology,* p. 110. Schnackenburg agrees that John's "Son of Man Christology" is a consistent unit (*The Gospel According to St. John, Vol. 1,* p. 532). A different view is maintained by E. D. Freed ("The Son of Man in the Fourth Gospel," *JBL,* 86 [1967], 402–409) but quite unconvincingly.

101. This is also, essentially, the position of Schnackenburg: the evangelist, he says, must have "himself adopted diverse traditions and worked them into his theology" (*The Gospel According to St. John, Vol. 1,* p. 71).

102. Cf. Brown, *The Gospel According to St. John,* p. 220; and M. E.

129

Boismard, "L'Évolution du thème eschatologique dans les traditions johanniques," *RB,* 68 (1961), 516.

103. *Ibid.*

104. Cf. Hoskyns, *op. cit.,* pp. 360–362; R. H. Lightfoot, *op. cit.,* pp. 16, 138, 201.

105. The *more* apparent difficulty for those unfamiliar with the background and current premises of New Testament exegesis is the assumed uncertainty on the part of the evangelist as to how to conceive of Jesus as divine. But, as noted in n. 83 above, a precisely constructed Christology is not to be expected from the New Testament, especially since, as Brown observes (*The Gospel According to St. John,* p. 24), "God" for the Jews meant the heavenly Father, and "until a wider understanding of the term was reached, it could not be readily applied to Jesus." In terms of biblical inspiration the presence of a twofold Christology is no more of a problem than the presence of a twofold eschatology (which is admitted by all). One is more representative of the evangelist's mature understanding than the other, but the latter is not eliminated because it contains a traditional element which called for integration. As we shall see, this the evangelist ultimately effected.

106. In the *Epistle to Diognetus,* attributed to Pantaenus (Clement of Alexandria's predecessor as director of the Christian school at Alexandria) by H. I. Marrou (*A Diognète, Sources Chrétiennes* [Paris, 1951], p. 266), the author makes this exact statement (x, 6–7). F. M. Braun (*op. cit.,* pp. 71–80) accepts Marrou's identification of the author and says of the passage in which the relevant statement is made that it contains a theology of agape (love) *"singulièrement apparentée à celle de la première épître de Jean ch. iv"* (p. 73).

107. An agraphon of the Lord reading: "Thou seest thy brother, thou seest thy God" is preserved by Clement of Alexandria (*Stromata,* 1, 19; 2, 15) and Tertullian (*De Oratione,* 26); its Johannine flavor is evident.

108. Cf. nn. 83 and 105 above.

109. *Adumbrationes in I Petri Epistulam* (*MPG,* 9, 729–730).

110. See the excursus at the end of Part Three.

111. Cf. E. Conze, "Buddhism and Gnosis," in *Le Origini dello Gnosticismo,* Suppl. Numen xii (Leiden, 1967), pp. 654–655. Such a view was adopted by some Mahayanists after 200 A.D. as a result of Gnostic influence, but it is "clearly a foreign body" in direct conflict with the basic Mahayanist tenet that the Buddha nature is the same in all.

112. E. Conze, *Selected Sayings from the Perfection of Wisdom* (London, ²1968), p. 116.

113. In the terms of Clement of Alexandria (cf. n. 82 above), the "understanding" given to us is not other than the Holy Spirit. Cf. F. Amiot, "Deum nemo vidit umquam Jo. 1, 19," in *Mélanges Robert* (Paris, 1956), pp. 470–477, esp. p. 473.

114. Conze, *Selected Sayings,* pp. 115–116.

115. See the excursus at the end of Part Three.

116. On this other fundamental Mahayanist concept, cf. F. J. Streng, *Emptiness: A Study in Religious Meaning* (Nashville, 1967); and B. L. Suzuki, *Mahayana Buddhism* (London, 1959), pp. 27–31.

117. This is another phrase employed by the author of the *Epistle to Diognetus:* "do not wonder that man can become an *imitator of God"* (x, 4).

118. Cf. n. 55 above.

119. J. L. Martyn, *op. cit.,* p. xi.

120. E. Stauffer, *New Testament Theology,* p. 42.

121. E. Käsemann, *The Testament of Jesus,* p. 2.

122. So also J. Dupont, *Essais sur la Christologie de S. Jean* (Bruges, 1951), pp. 37–39; and T. F. Glasson, *op. cit.,* pp. 86–88.

123. *The Gospel According to St. John,* p. 91.

124. At Jn. 1, 15. 30, the Baptist makes a statement about Jesus which is difficult to interpret. In one view it is a reference to the pre-existence of Jesus; in another it is an allusion to Elijah; and in a third, it simply means: "There is a man in my following who has superseded me because he is and always has been my superior." Cf. Brown, *The Gospel According to St. John,* p. 64; J. A. T. Robinson, *Twelve New Testament Studies* (London, 1962), pp. 28–52; C. H. Dodd, *Historical Tradition in the Fourth Gospel* (Cambridge, 1963), p. 274. Given the variety of possible interpretations of this statement, we shall prescind from consideration of it here.

125. *Ad Autolycum,* II, 22. If Irenaeus (*Adv. Haeres.,* I, 8, 5) is quoting verbatim, as seems to be the case, then the Gnostic Ptolemy also explicitly referred to the fourth gospel as "John's." This testimony would be more or less contemporaneous with that of Theophilus of Antioch, perhaps a decade earlier.

126. C. H. Dodd, "The Prophecy of Caiaphas," *NovT,* Suppl. vi (Leiden, 1962), 134–143.

127. This is also another instance of John's selection of a detail for its symbolic value. Huge quantities of spices were a feature of royal obsequies (Jer. 34, 5; Fl. Josephus, *Antiquities,* XVII, 8) and Jesus is a king (see also my article cited in n. 52 above). Only a very rich man like Nicodemus could pay homage of this sort to Jesus.

128. Cf. Schnackenburg, *The Gospel According to St. John, Vol. 1,* p. 365 n. 57.

129. *The Gospel History and Its Transmission* (Edinburgh, 1911), p. 250.

130. As Dodd in all his work has shown it to be. Cf. especially his *The Parables of the Kingdom* (London, rev. ed., 1961).

131. Cf. J. Bonsirven, "Les Aramaismes de S. Jean l'Evangeliste?" *Bibl,* 30 (1949), 405–432.

132. C. F. Burney, *The Aramaic Origin of the Fourth Gospel* (London, 1922); C. C. Torrey, "The Aramaic Origin of the Gospel of John,"

HarvTR, 16 (1923), 305–344. Cf. S. Brown, "From Burney to Black: The Fourth Gospel and the Aramaic Question," *CBQ,* 26 (1964), 323–339.

133. Cf. C. H. Dodd, *The Interpretation of the Fourth Gospel* p. 75.

134. Cf. Sanders and Mastin, *op. cit.,* p. 412, esp. n. 3; Schnackenburg, *The Gospel According to St. John, Vol. 1,* pp. 93–94.

135. *Ibid.*

136. Cf. F. C. Grant, *First John, Nelson's Bible Commentary,* vol. 7 (New York, 1962), p. 349. The metric character of the verse is noticed by Schnackenburg (*Die Johannesbriefe* [Freiburg, 1963], p. 50).

137. So, e.g., F. C. Grant, *The Gospels, Their Origin and Their Growth* (London, 1957), pp. 159–106.

138. In general, Schnackenburg (*The Gospel According to St. John, Vol. 1,* 128–135) shows himself quite reserved about accepting any direct influence from Qumran on John, and it is to be hoped that his attitude heralds a trend away from the frenetic compulsion to find all sorts of links between the two. It seems to me that only a kind of insensitivity to the difference in spirit between the Johannine writings and that of Qumran can account for the illusion of a real affinity between them.

139. Cf. M. Mansoor, "The Nature of Gnosticism in Qumran," in *Le Origini dello Gnosticismo,* pp. 389–400, esp. p. 391.

140. *Gnosis and the New Testament* (Oxford, 1968), p. 46.

141. According to Cerinthus, as recounted by Irenaeus (*Adv. Haeres, I,* 26, 1), "the Christ" descended on Jesus in the form of a dove at the moment of Jesus' baptism but departed from him before the crucifixion. Hence John states: "Jesus Christ, not with the water only, but with the water and the blood." Many have seen in this verse an allusion to Jn. 19, 34, but this is very uncertain (cf. A. E. Brooke, *op. cit.,* pp. 131–134).

142. Cf. Dodd, *The Johannine Epistles,* pp. 58ff. Hippolytus (*Philosophoumena,* V. 9. 121–122) quotes certain Gnostics as saying: "We alone of all men are Christians . . . anointed . . . with the speechless chrism."

143. Cf. Brooke, *op. cit.,* pp. xlv–xlix; Wilson, *op. cit.,* p. 40.

144. Addressed as "elect lady"; the presbyter ends the short letter: "the children of your sister, the elect [lady] greet you." There is no question of actual women intended here. We find an almost exact parallel in 1 Peter (5, 13) which concludes: "the co-elect [lady] in Babylon greets you." The *Pastor Hermae* calls the Church "the lady" (Vis I, 2, 2; 2, 1, 3).

145. This is why Schnackenburg's otherwise interesting reconstruction of the background of the two small epistles ("Der Streit zwischen dem Verfasser von 3 Joh und Diotrephes und seine verfassungsgeschichtliche Bedeutung," *MüTZ,* 4 [1953], 18–26) must be rejected.

146. *Adv. Haeres,* III, 1, 2; II, 33, 3; III, 11, 7. 3. Eusebius, *Hist. Eccl.,* V, 20.

147. Acts 14, 14; cf. also 2 Cor. 8, 23; Rom. 16, 7; Phil. 2, 25.

148. Most scholars are confident that Polycrates has here confused Philip the apostle with Philip the deacon, whose daughters are mentioned in Acts 21, 8–9.

149. The letter of Polycrates to Victor was preserved by Eusebius (*Hist. Eccl.*, III, 31; V. 24). The "petalon" was a gold ornament worn on the priestly turban and inscribed with the words: "Holy to Yahweh" (Ex. 28, 36–38).

150. Cf. Schnackenburg (*The Gospel According to St. John, Vol. 1*, p. 83). In his interesting analysis of this fragment, A. Resch suggested that the words *ex decipolis* (usually rendered as "of the disciples") are a barbarous transliteration of the Greek *ek dekapoleos,* which, if so, would witness to a tradition that the fourth gospel was written in one of the cities of the Decapolis, probably Pella (*Aussercanonische Paralleltexte zu den Evangelien* [TU, 10, 1896; IV, 32–33]), a suggestion which has never, to my knowledge, been given due consideration.

151. Preserved by Eusebius (*Hist. Eccl.*, III, 23).

152. *Adv. Marcion.*, IV, 2.

153. *De Praescr. Haer.*, 36, 3.

154. *Philosophoumena,* VII, 33, 1; X, 21. M. G. Bardy ("Cérinthe," *RB,* 30 [1921], 344–373) is inclined to discount this information, but for no sufficient reason, given the breadth of Hippolytus' knowledge. In sharp contrast to the tradition that John the evangelist was an outspoken critic of Cerinthus is another, well attested tradition, initiated, it would seem, by the late-second-century Roman presbyter Gaius, that Cerinthus was himself the author of the fourth gospel! Cf. Epiphanius, *Haer.,* 51, 1 (*MPG,* 41, 888ff.); Philastrius, *Diversarum Haer.,* 60 (*CSEL,* 38, 31f.). Dionysius Bar Salibi (*In Apocalypsim* [*CSCO,* 2d series, 101, 1–2]) cites Hippolytus as a witness to and opponent of the views of Gaius.

155. B. P. W. Stather-Hunt (*Some Johannine Problems* [London, 1958]) makes very much of this in arguing for Alexandria as the place of composition (pp. 97–104, 113, 119). For different reasons, J. L. Martyn (*op. cit.,* p. 58 n. 94) is the most recent proponent of the Alexandrian origin of the gospel.

156. *Lettres et écrivains chrétiens des IIe et IIIe siècles* (Paris, 1961), pp. 69–70.

157. An interpretation favored by Braun (*op. cit., pp.* 339f.), and Schnackenburg (*The Gospel According to St. John, Vol. 1,* p. 81).

158. The Greek *"martus"* can mean both "witness" and "martyr" depending upon the context. There is some evidence that John the son of Zebedee was put to death together with his brother James (Acts 12, 2), chiefly an alleged statement by Papias to that effect recorded by the epitomist of the Chronicle of Philip of Side (a mediocre Church historian of the fifth century) and some martyrologies (Syriac and Armenian) of the fourth and fifth centuries. None of this information is treated very seriously today, though new discoveries might rehabilitate it

in the future. In any case, it may be that Polycrates, who almost certainly considered the John of Ephesus to be the son of Zebedee (mistakenly, I believe), was aware of this tradition, or that the John buried in his city (John Mark, I believe) was a martyr.

159. Cf. G. W. Butterworth, "The Story of St. John and the Robber," *JTS*, 18 (1916–1917), 141–146.

160. Not a new view. J. Wellhausen identified John Mark with the beloved disciple at the turn of the century (*Das Evangelium Johannis* [Berlin, 1908], pp. 87ff.) More recently, it has been defended by Pierson Parker ("John and John Mark," *JBL*, 79 [1960], 97–110) and J. N. Sanders (*op. cit.*, pp. 44–52, and much more fully in earlier articles).

161. Cf. M. J. Routh, *Reliquiae Sacrae II*, p. 28. Other witnesses are the Monarchian prologue to the second gospel (cf. De Bruyne, *art. cit.*, 204) and the Venerable Bede (*Expositio in Marci Evangelium*, Epist. ad Accam. [*MPL*, 92, 133]).

162. I, 9–10, 13–16; II, 4. The Clementine literature dates from the first decades of the third century.

163. *Ante-Nicene Library*, XVI (Edinburgh, 1870), pp. 293–300. The editor notes that the book has more "an air of truth about it" than others in its class. This opinion still prevails. The *Acts of Barnabas* dates no later than the fifth century and shows that the author knew Cyprus well.

164. The pastoral epistles, in the form in which we have them, are not considered today as coming from the hand of the apostle but rather from a "Pauline circle." However, with regard to 2 Tim. 4, 11, V. Taylor (*The Gospel According to St. Mark* [London, 1954], p. 29), who is representative of the best critical opinion, says: "The last Pauline reference to Mark is in the genuine note embedded in 2 Timothy iv, 11." Interestingly, Dom Calmet took it for granted that the John buried at Ephesus was John Mark (*Dictionarium Historicum Criticum Sacrae Scripturae I* [Venice, 1766], p. 502).

165. Cf. Eusebius (*Hist. Eccl.*, VII, 25). Dionysius says of Mark that "it is not written that he went with them [Barnabas and Paul] into Asia," taking no account of Col. 4, 10 or 2 Tim. 4, 11.

166. *In Acta Ap. Hom. XXVI* (*MPG*, 60, 201).

167. Cf. *Acta Sanctorum Martii II* (Paris and Rome, 1856), p. 369. The Spanish writers identify "Aristobulus, the brother of Barnabas," and the father of John Mark according to Eastern traditions (cf. n. 173 below), with Zebedee, the father of James and John the apostles.

168. Cf. n. 32 above. According to the account given in *The New York Times*, this letter testifies to Mark's presence in Alexandria. If genuine, it becomes the earliest witness to this tradition.

169. Cf. J. E. Bruns, "John Mark: A Riddle within the Johannine Enigma," *Script*, 15 (1963), 88–92; and "The Confusion between John and John Mark in Antiquity," *Script*, 17 (1965), 23–26.

170. Perhaps John Mark *is* Mark the evangelist and also John the evangelist (cf. n. 179 below), but as the passage from Dionysius of Alex-

andria shows, neither identification was known to him. Mark the evangelist emerges as a personality in his own right (cf. n. 176 below), to which at a later date the mantle of John Mark is added. As suggested in the text, the reason for the dissociation of John Mark with either gospel must be sought in the ambiguous position to which his falling-out with Paul had relegated him.

171. *MPG*, 87, iii, 4091–4099.

172. The author states at one point that he is giving what the "holy fathers" said.

173. *History of the Patriarchs of Alexandria*, pt. 1, ch. 1 (*PO*, 1, 135ff.), a tenth-century compilation and translation of Greek and Coptic fragments which depend heavily upon Eusebius and certain early *Acts*. The narrative introduces John Mark as one of those who "poured out the water which our Lord turned into wine at the marriage of Cana in Galilee."

174. E.g., F. C. Grant, *The Earliest Gospel* (Nashville, 1943), pp. 34–57, esp. pp. 52–57.

175. Cf. n. 161 above.

176. Cf. Eusebius (*Hist. Eccles.*, III, 39). In the Muratorian canon Hippolytus(?) says of Luke: "neither did he see the Lord in the flesh," implying that the previous evangelist (Mark) had not done so either. Only part of the final sentence regarding the second gospel is extant in the text.

177. Jerome merely says that he "thinks" John Mark is the second evangelist (*In Epist. ad Philem.* [*MPL*, 23, 763]).

178. Cf. *Acta Sanctorum*, xlvii (Sept. t. vii), 354; the feast day observed is September 27th.

179. Cf. H. L. Jackson, *op. cit.*, pp. 108–109.

180. *Dialogue with Trypho*, 81 (*MPG*, 6, 669). This dialogue took place in Ephesus (Eusebius, *Hist. Eccl.*, IV, 18).

181. He refers to this John as one who had been "in the midst" of the citizens of Ephesus (i.e., of the audience he was addressing).

182. Cf. A. Wikenhauser, *New Testament Introduction* (New York, 1963), pp. 548–551.

183. *Constitutiones Apostolorum*, VII, 46. Recording the succession of bishops, it reads: "At Ephesus: Timothy [appointed] by Paul; John [appointed] by me, John."

184. The passage is preserved by Eusebius (*Hist. Eccl.*, III, 39).

185. Preserved by Irenaeus (*Adv. Haer.*, V, 33, 3).

186. A. Farrer has carefully illustrated the similarities; cf. his *The Revelation of St. John the Divine* (Oxford, 1964), pp. 41–50.

187. Cf. R. McL. Wilson, *op. cit.*, pp. 15–16. The student has to deal separately with pre-Christian Gnosis, with the second-century Christian heresy which we call "Gnosticism," with Manicheism, with Mandaism, with Jewish Kabbalism, and with such medieval sects as the Bogomils, the Cathari, and the Albigensians.

188. Cf. L. Tondelli, *Gnostici* (Turin, 1950). Gnosticism, he says,

following Buonaiuti, was a movement which developed *"nelle due grandî città intellettuali dei primi tre secoli cristiani, Alessandria e Roma"* (p. 45).

189. Cf. C. J. Bleeker, "The Egyptian Background of Gnosticism," in *Le Origini dello Gnosticismo,* pp. 229f.

190. Cf. Wilson, *op. cit.,* p. 16 n. 36. Wilson would be in favor of adopting Munck's suggestion that Gnosis in the wider sense be termed "syncretism" were it not for the fact that "syncretism" is already used in two distinct though related senses.

191. Cf. J. Doresse, *The Secret Books of the Egyptian Gnostics* (New York, 1960), pp. 284–285; G. Woodcock, *The Greeks in India* (London, 1966) pp. 157–158; Wilson, *op. cit.,* p. 13; E. Conze, "Buddhism and Gnosis," pp. 651–667. An early work is that of J. Kennedy, "Buddhist Gnosticism: The System of Basilides," in *JRAS* (1902), 377–415.

192. *Ibid.*

193. Pp. 665–667; Wilson, *ibid;* Doresse, *ibid.*

194. The archaeological evidence was reported by Flinders Petrie in *Man,* 8 (1908), 129. Cf. also D. R. Bhandarkar, "Asoka and His Successors," in *A Comprehensive History of India,* K. A. N. Shastri (ed.), II (Bombay, 1957), p. 40; and G. Woodcock, *op. cit.,* p. 156.

195. Cf. J. Filliozat, "Les échanges de l'Inde et de l'empire romain aux premiers siècles de l'ère chrétienne," *Revue Historique,* 201 (1949), 1–29, esp. 6.

196. *Oratio XXXII ad Alexandrinos* (Loeb Library, Dio Chrysostom, III, 211).

197. *Art. cit.,* 27–29. He writes that Hippolytus had before him a *recent* document of remarkable precision: *"de source récente et dont l'exactitude est remarquable."* The text of Hippolytus is in his *Philosophoumena* 1, 24 (*MPG,* XVI, iii, 44ff.), which was written about 222 A.D. Cf. also J. Filliozat: "La doctrine des brahmanes d'après saint Hippolyte," *Revue de l'Hist. des Rel.* (1945), 59–91.

198. Cf. J. Quasten, *Patrology, II* (Westminster, Md., 1953), p. 163. Quasten writes: "His theological attitude and the relation of his doctrine of the Logos to that of the Greek theologians prove his Hellenistic training and connection with Alexandria."

199. Cf. E. Conze, "The Mahayana," in *Concise Encyclopedia of Living Faiths,* R. C. Zaehner (ed.) (Boston, 1967), pp. 296–297. The parallel in the *Perfection of Wisdom* is with Rev. 5, 1–9.

200. Eusebius, *Hist. Eccl.,* V, 10, 3; Jerome, *De viris illustribus,* 36. The details given by Jerome are not suggestive of a mere legend.

201. Pantaenus is often called the "founder" of the Christian school at Alexandria, but according to a fragment of Philip of Side, the founder of the school was Athenagoras, to whom Pantaenus succeeded (cf. *MPG,* 39, 229).

202. Jerome, *Epistola lxxiv* (ad Magnum).

203. Clement of Alexandria, *Stromata,* 1, 15; 3, 7. Cf. H. de Lubac,

Aspects of Buddhism (London, 1953), p. 164. Woodcock (*op. cit.*, p. 157) notes that Clement's transliteration of "Boutta" shows more regard for accurate phonetics than that of modern Europeans.

204. Set forth in detail by de Lubac in *Aspects of Buddhism,* pp. 86–115. See also by the same author, "Textes Alexandrins et Bouddhiques," *RechSR,* 27 (1937), 336–351.

205. *Ibid.,* 351.

206. Cf. E. Benz, *Indische Einflüsse auf die frühchristliche Theologie* (Akad. Wiss. u. Lit. Mainz, rev. 1951, no. 3), esp. pp. 197–202.

207. H. Cornelis, "The Resurrection of the Body: The Teaching of the Fathers," in *The Resurrection of the Body* (Notre Dame, 1964), pp. 123–199.

208. *Ibid.,* p. 185. Gregory of Nyssa defines corporeality as a simple conjunction of qualities, a mere conglomerate of moral and physical dispositions. This is the Buddhist view of man's individuality.

Indexes

Index of Biblical References

141

Index of Other Ancient Sources

147

Index of Modern Authors

151